Introduction

Over the last couple of years, a lot of people have asked me "Brian, why do you love God so much?" The question that really should be asked is "Why does God love me?" The problem with that question for me was that for most of my life, I couldn't answer that question with true honesty. I had what I thought was a fairly decent relationship with our LORD but I was completely wrong. I thought that just because I went to church, prayed and did what was right, I was to have an automatic entrance into eternal glory. Wouldn't it have been so much easier and pleasurable to be able to just do what I want, be who I want and really live my life the way I WANT? Throughout my life, I had listened to what everyone else was telling me instead of trusting in the LORD and coming to him for guidance. In this book, I want to share with you the power of God's grace and mercy through my experiences and hopefully make you aware that our God is a faithful and loving father. This journey you have chosen to embark on will take you on the path through my "garden" that God has created for me and the unforeseen challenges that arose. Throughout my readings of the Bible, I have come across a very powerful message found in *Matthew Chapter 13;* the parable of the Seed and Sower. The four seeds mentioned are as follows. First is the one by the wayside. Think of yourself as the seed. You were planted, either in a ditch or poor soil, meaning that you heard God's word but didn't understand it. The second is the seed on the stone surface where you here the word and receive it but has no root and stumbles in trouble. The third seed is the seed planted amongst thorns. This is where you hear the world but cares for the worldly stuff so you "chokes". And last but not least is the seed planted in good soil where you hear the word, receive it and live it. I firmly believe what it says in *Galatians 6:7-You Reap What You Sow.*

As I sit here typing this, I can't help but reflect on the challenges that have surfaced since I gave my life to Christ nearly three years ago. I thought of all my problems that were swept under the rug or forgotten about but making that decision to walk with Christ brought them all to the surface. I see now that I am reaping what I have sowed. The good thing about God is He is a loving and forgiving father so even though the problems surfaced, He helped me through them just like a father helps his son overcome adversary. Looking back, I planted some terrible seeds, but I was also able to plant some of the most fruitful seeds God could provide. One seed in particular that has ended up being not only a bad seed but also a good seed was the seed planted with my marriage. You see all four seeds individually shaped my life but the seed of my marriage was regrettably a combination of them all. Unfortunately though, I had no idea how to "maintain and cultivate a prosperous garden." Only as my seeds were destroyed was I able to finally submit myself to God's grace and allow him to work through me. My journey on the path that God has paved for me has taken me to some absolutely amazing places but through my own disobedience, I have also been to some horrific places. During this journey, God still loved me enough to provide me with multiple ways out, a great selection of fellow Christians to help me and opportunities to help others along the way. As much as I thought I loved God, I still refused to listen and decided to take the easy way out of everything. Wouldn't you agree that doing things your own way is so much easier and pleasurable? I certainly thought so. Boy was I wrong and God, lovingly and respectfully, let me do my own thing because of free will. Sounds like a dream come true doesn't it? Well you tell me…

Chapter One

My parents, at the time of my conception, weren't truly ready for what God had blessed them with. Now don't get me wrong, my dad was a good man and provided for me and my two younger brothers but one thing was missing, love. My biological mom was so young at the time when I we were conceived, that she herself was still a child. This combination of the lack of love and the immaturity posed for a disastrous combination for the three of us. For the first part of my life, while my biological mom was still around, all I can remember is being exposed to a large selection of drugs and multiple men coming in and out on a daily basis. What made this terrible was that I thought this was an acceptable thing so I never mentioned it to my dad. My recollection of life began in the spring of 1990 and my brothers and I were sitting watching TV just like any other day. All of a sudden, there was a loud knock at the door and two individuals, who were dressed really well, came inside. I later learned that they were from the Department of Social Services. After a few minutes speaking to my father, the two individuals came to us and asked us if we were ready to go. My dad bent down to our eye level and gave all three of us huge hugs with tears streaming down his face and as clear as day he said "I love you guys I am going to figure this all out really soon I promise". See because of the lack of parental guidance, someone had called social services and they deemed it necessary that this current living situation wasn't conducive to our well-being. There was absolutely nothing my dad could do at the time because he was working so much to provide for us and my biological mom wasn't ever around or in the right mindset to be a parent. These circumstances put us into the custody of the State of Pennsylvania until further notice. Over the next few months, we were switched from foster home to foster home, and at times, separated from each other. From what I can remember, the families we were placed with were nice to us but the lack of love still wasn't there. Every night, one of us, if not all three of us, would lay up crying for our dad. Even at a young age, I can sense that all of this was visibly frustrating to the families that took us in. There was this one particular family who locked me and my middle brother up in a room all day. They only came in twice to feed us but paid no attention to my brother's diapers. Well, being the brazen boy he was at the time, my brother took out his feces and smeared it all over the wall. When the parents came in, they took him and whooped his behind repeatedly. The next day, we were back in custody of Social Services. Now grant it my brothers and I weren't bad but just think about the behaviors of children with no guidance at all? After this moment we were placed in another home but this time all three of us were together again. Finally, we at least had each other even if no one else wanted us.

Over the next few days, I was sensing that the effects this all was having on my brothers was getting to them. I even got to the point where I began questioning God on all of this. "God what's your problem?" I ask. "This isn't fair and it's not right" as I remember laying in my bed hurting because I couldn't stop the pain that was coming from my brothers. I began to doubt myself as a big brother and my life suddenly hit fast forward so instead of being that six year old, I had to quickly grow up and take care of my brothers not having a clue on what to do. About two weeks into this new stay, the same two Social Service individuals who took us from our dad came for us again. I remember my youngest brother Clyde tugging on the Social Service workers pant leg asking her "Why are you here?" The lady then got down to his level and said "I came to get you and your brothers. You are going home to your dad". I won't forget that moment for the rest of my life. Both my brothers came running to me, almost knocking me over, and we all hugged tightly with tears streaming from our eyes. At this time I didn't know it but God had delivered us a miracle.

Walking into that office that day and seeing my father that day still gets me choked up. Now you would have thought we all would have been elated to see him but we weren't. We were scared. As we proceeded through the office, we see our father with a woman who we had never met and we began to think "Oh no, where is Mommy?" When we had reached our dad, he got down and gave us all really big hugs and told us he missed us a lot. He then proceeded to introduce to us this new person as his girlfriend and I looked at him and asked him "Where's Mommy?" For a moment a dead silence filled the room and my dad looked at his new girlfriend, then to us, and said "Boys, mommy left and she's never coming back. She has a new life but don't worry, we got each other and that's all that matters". Being so young, the absence of my mother really hit me hard and I began to muster resentment toward any female authority including my dad's new girlfriend. Surprisingly though, his new girlfriend was so kind and loving to us that we weren't sure how to react at the time and you could tell she knew it. Arriving at our new house, in the heart of the Coal Region in Pennsylvania, the vibe was nothing like I had ever felt before and still can't even describe them. In the back of my mind, I was still hurting from being sent away and having to "grow up" faster than I was ready to. The next few months were a huge challenge for all of us, including my dad and his girlfriend. "Who do you think you are that you can just come and replace my mommy?" I would always ask her. You know what though, she would always say "I will never replace your mom but I will always love you and be there for you as long as you let me". Surprisingly enough, that very answer broke down any walls that surrounded my heart. She knew that I would always have a place in my heart for my mom and unbeknownst to me, she would continue to love all of us

even through all of this.

Chapter 2

The new start gave all three of us a second chance to truly feel what family was all about. My dad was still working constantly providing for us and his new live-in girlfriend, who we were now suppose to call mom, even though we didn't want to, was there in his absence. One of the things about her that started chipping away at the wall of my heart was that in addition to being our new mom she really seemed to want to take care of us. No matter what the circumstance, she was always home when we got back from school and showed us love the best way she knew how. My goodness, after a few weeks and a lot of shed tears from the hurtful stuff we said to her about not being our mom, she never had stopped loving us. Even to this day, as an adult, I still don't understand why she cares for us like she does. Eventually, she earned the title MOM and will never relinquish that as long as I live. Now you would have thought that was the fairy tale ending we all wanted to hear after the rough start but there was no fairy tale. Something was going on in our family dynamic but I didn't know what. There was still something not right, something still missing. Luckily for me, I was personally blessed from God with being able to spend a great majority of my time with two amazing ladies. These ladies were extremely God-Fearing and tried to instill those same values in me. You might call them Mary and Sister Edna but I call them family. Let me tell you what. I have no idea what I did to deserve them, but growing up, they were my guardian angels. My relationship with God wasn't exactly a relationship though. When I was with my gram and Sister Edna, God was always the main focus. We would go to service at least once a week and even while watching tv or eating, God was still the center of most of our discussions, just as he should always be. When I was living with my father and mother however, God was known but hardly ever mentioned. We would go to service periodically but even then there was no enthusiasm for God. This began to start a mass confusion for me and I ended up deciding to take the easy way out and not strengthen my relationship with God that I had later desired to have. Not only did I not understand anything about him, I just didn't care. While at home, I was seeing people come and go, so the idea of starting or maintaining a relationship became pointless. I mean logically think about it, seeing this on a daily basis why not get what you want and move on. No sense to keep anyone around right?

As I have and will continue to mention, my father was an incredible man. No matter what he had to do, there was always food on the table, clothes on our backs and the bills were paid. Regrettably, because of his colossal work ethic, it took away from him spending quality time with us. Growing up, I had a huge resentment to him because of this but was always afraid to express myself. It was an engrained from day one that "men don't cry and they don't express themselves to anyone." I always felt like I was a burden to him and my mom. You know I look back at those years and would much rather be broke, living on the streets with nothing but the clothes on my back just to know that I wasn't a burden to them. You see because of the morals and values that were provided to me from Sister Edna and my gram, I very easily flew under the radar. Really, I can't remember a single instance where someone cared enough to ask me "How my day was" or wanted to know where I was or how things were going. It is a very safe assumption to know that yes I was the good kid and that's why people didn't feel the need to check up on me. Throughout the years I continually asked "God where were you? You claim to love me and I do my best at being a good kid but you gave me this life and these circumstances?" So by this point, I completely stopped caring about God and began doing what I wanted. Meanwhile to appease my gram and

Sister Edna, I would know just enough about God to fake that I cared. What I didn't see was at this time, God, through the both of them, had allowed me through free will to plant the first seeds in my life.

I can always remember going to see my gram and Sister Edna and seeing how they tried to ingrain the teachings of God and Bible to me. I began seeing how they were living their lives according to God and it started rubbing off on me and my parents that we started becoming more active in the church. Would you believe that later in life they both thought I would become a preacher? Isn't that something to sleep on? So anyways, my brothers and I got transferred to a catholic school for not only a better education but to learn more about God. My catholic school experience was horrible, however, not because of the lessons but because of the actions of others. I distinctively remember walking into my 4th grade classroom for the first time at the ripe age of ten and seeing my first crush, let's just call her Ms. Sunday. When I walked into that classroom, I prayed that I would sit close to her and maybe muster the courage to eventually talk to her. This sounds so lame but even at ten years old, this girl was so beautiful. She had dark hair, smooth skin and a smile that could distract anyone from what they were doing. For the next three years, I learned a lot of valuable things pertaining to God and the Bible. I learned, but sort of didn't believe, that he loved me unconditionally no matter what I did. I began to slowly try and bring down my wall but no matter how hard I tried, the challenges that arose really prevented any progress. The most difficult of it all was having to face my crush every day for three years. No matter what I did or said, she and her friends ridiculed and made fun of me so I shut down and became resentful to women because all are alike right? I tried every day to just talk to her, be respectful, but she would blow me off like I was a virus. I can remember a specific incident that I believe started what would end up being years of anger and resentment towards women. We were at a school dance and at this time, one of the most popular slow dance songs was *"I Swear by All for One"*. I actually had the courage that day to ask her that if that song should play, that I'd like to have the pleasure of dancing with her. You know what she said, believe it or not she said "YES". Boy was I ecstatic because all these years of trying and hoping was worth the wait just for this one dance. About an hour into the dance, the song came on so I went to look for her and as clear as day, I can still see her and her friends at the top of the steps looking and laughing at me while pointing their fingers. Not even a few seconds later, she was dancing with someone else to this same exact song and it crushed me. I walked out of that dance that night holding everything in. Walking home by myself, I decided to let it all out in a flurry of tears that completely overwhelmed me. I was so devastated and couldn't think of what I had possibly done to deserve that. After that day, I just gave up.

In order to combat the hurt, I decided to join the school's basketball team and actually did fairly well. My only problem with that was that no one knew how well I was doing. My family didn't come to hardly any of my games and I had to rely on others for rides to other schools. Think about how that felt seeing other parents love on their child, saying "they are proud" but here I am waiting outside with no one! The only bright side I had experienced in catholic school was that I had an amazing 4th grader teacher, Mrs. Rodgers, who treated me like a son. As luck would have it, Mrs. Rodgers also lived a block from my grams and was very good friends with her. I distinctly remember I decided to run away from home for a few days but when I eventually returned, she was there with open arms. I don't remember exactly what transpired, all I could remember was that she told me that she loved me and would never give up on me no matter what. Eventually I had to graduate from the 4th grade and didn't get to see much of her anymore after that. I learned at a very young age that people are like seasons, they come and go so why care about anyone. They will just be gone the next day won't they? As the years passed, the anger and jokes started to take an even bigger toll on me than I could handle. I was in the 6th grade and my computer teacher was making fun of me just like everyone else was so I fought back, not physically but verbally. Do you know what happened? He slammed me against the wall in the principal's office then I was expelled the same day. The worst part of it all was that when my mom had picked me up, she didn't discipline me, she told me I had to face my gram and tell her what I did. That, to me, was the worst thing because my gram loved me so much and I didn't want to let her down like I thought I was to everyone else. I was surprised to experience that she didn't just forgive me, she helped me overcome it. That whole day all we talked about was forgiveness and she showed me in the Book of Matthew and Ephesians that God loves me even though I messed up. As much as I was listening, I still wasn't having it. I was just expelled from school, where was God's love then?

CHAPTER 3

After my expulsion, I was forced back into the public school system where my problems just followed me just with different characters but even more resentment. At this point in my life, the effects of what Sister Edna and my gram were having on me began putting small cracks in the walls I had around my heart. My heart was still hurting from my first crush but as time faded, so did the feelings. I was able to focus more on school and being a kid then what she or any others thought about me. What was kind of ironic was that Ms. Sunday transferred to public school shortly after I had. Her first few days she began to realize she wasn't Ms. Popular here so who do you think she came to? Now what did I do you may ask? I did exactly what she deserved to get, my kindness and respect. What's even more ironic, was after the fact when she got some friends and seen me in the halls, she acted like she didn't even know me. You know I sat in my room for a week angry and yelling to God, "why wasn't I good enough". She hurt me so much emotionally and psychologically that I couldn't accept anything anyone ever said. How did I know it wasn't going to happen again? What did I ever do to her? Again I had let my guard down and was steamrolled. This constant ridicule and rejection started to heat up inside me and because of that I never fit into any specific clique. I was what you'd call a loner. Even at home, I didn't feel like I belonged. I began to fall into the dangerous cycle of pornography because it helped me feel good about myself. In the real world, I couldn't have the girl I wanted so why not just settle for the other option. Self-medication was almost a daily thing for me and no one even asked questions because I could hide things easily. Adding insult to injury, did my parents ever ask "How was I doing?" Nope they didn't, they were caught up in other things more important and I never understood what's more important than your child. Instead of facing my fears, I learned to run and running I did.

In the beginning of my 9th grade year, my parents decided to move us to a new town to be closer to their jobs which I was half ecstatic and half confused about it. The best thing about the move was that my dad would be around more often which meant more to me than any person I'd be leaving behind. Before I left, I wanted to make sure I said goodbye to a certain few, one in particular, who was a about a year older than me but probably the sweetest person I had met not part of my family. When I stopped to say goodbye, I actually teared up because she told me that I was truly going to miss me and that I was a really good person. What caught me off guard was that after I gave her a hug she gave me a peck on the cheek and wished me the best. Why would a popular cheerleader even care about dorky little me? I was so happy she cared enough about me but in the back of my mind all I can think of was "did she have an ulterior motive or did she actually care? I never understood why my parents would take us from an environment we were use to, especially for me in my freshman year of high school. To make matters worse, we moved to the rival school, so I already had a black mark against me. My first few days at the new school actually went by way better than anticipated. Yes, I was busted on but it was truly out of good fun. Man I can remember working in the elementary library one day with three other classmates, one of whom was so beautiful I couldn't even look her in the eyes. At that time in my life, I enjoyed singing and actually was attempting to make a career out of it so I told her about it and she wanted me to sing to her. I didn't think anything of it and the next day I sang to her. To my surprise, she genuinely smiled at me and had a tear in her eye. The star quarterback of our class came up to me and told me that she really liked me and wanted me to ask her out. I was a huge jerk though and blew her off because I assumed she was going to be like everyone else. I assumed that after I asked her out she would make a fool out of me just like Ms. Sunday did. I always thought that I was the brunt of everyone's jokes and refused to allow myself to be subjected to this again or ever for that matter. What made matters worse was the fact that this school was really hard on "outsiders" so on top of the wall being up , I just always assumed the worst when people were trying to be nice, especially the popular kids. I did however have a very small select group of friends which made my high school life bearable. I hated my new school more than life itself. You know the majority of the staff didn't really care about what I did either. For a good portion of my high school life, I slept in nearly every class. The only ones I didn't sleep in were with teachers I believed actually cared for us more than just students. I still have two teachers to this day who keep in contact with me via social media and actually ask "How am I doing". Now that's a teacher! Don't get me wrong not everyone treated me harshly but that's only because I didn't associate myself with many of them. Surprisingly, I later had found out that two girls in my high school actually had a crush on me but I blew them off because I was trying to disassociate myself with anything related to that school

Things started to look promising for me at the age of 17. I was living any guy's dream. I had tons of female friends in my life. I knew everything there was to know about a female except how to get them to see me more as a boyfriend. I was the good guy, the best friend, but that's all I ever was. Day in and day out, I would be contacted by a females looking for advice or a shoulder to cry on. At this point in my life, I knew more about a female then most females knew about themselves. This became a dangerous combination later in life but at this moment it helped out a lot because it led me to my greatest memory but biggest mistake I had made growing up. I started working my first job, like any other kid at the time, at McDonalds. This would be where I would meet this super awesome, amazing, beautiful young lady named Shelia who happened to be the trainer at the time. When we locked eyes, and what's funny is I can still visualize this, I knew I had to try. The store manager strategically placed me with her and I seriously was so happy she did because it gave me the door I needed to at least have a conversation. The first hour or so was all business but then I remember lightly squirting her hand with ketchup and giving a flirty smile. The most awesome thing transpired; she poked me in the side and I knew I had a chance from there. Throughout the rest of that shift, I could have cared less what I learned but when the day was over, I took the chance and guess what, she said yes. Can you believe that? Every time we were together we had the most amazing time. She even convinced me, and even to this day I don't know how, to go see an animated movie. When we went in and I saw that more than half the theater was screaming little kids I was speechless. I was thinking to myself, "so much for being romantic" but I could tell she was happy so I went with it. This girl was so smart and cute, funny and had such a strong heart that I didn't know how to act. I was so lost that I started to listen to what other people were saying. I had received two messages from people who I later learned were her friends telling me I was too good for her and all this garbage. I listened to these people because I thought they were my friends but I had learned they weren't and that they didn't want her to be with me. After about a month, I ended it all of a sudden and regretfully I didn't see or hear from her until years later when it was too late for the both of us. I was blessed to be associated with her and thanks to social media, I was able to eventually ask for her forgiveness which was all I ever wanted.

The only other good memory I had of growing up was that my brothers and I really enjoyed partaking in the local pool, teen night club and basketball courts. One day on our way home, we had seen this group of guys and one girl shooting around so we went for a pick up game. The girl that was there kept eyeing me down so I chose to cover her and do a little flirting. During the game, I was so distracted that when my brother passed me the ball, I missed it because all my focus was on this girl. After the game ended, she came up to me and told me I was cute and wrote her number on my hand. I looked at my brothers like, what in the world just happened? Over the next few months we became inseparable but just as friends. One day I felt confident enough to ask her out and she said the most hurtful thing I had ever heard at the time and what eventually became my signature. "I'm sorry Brian, but we are too good as friends". To this day, I cringe at hearing those words. I didn't know it at the time, but this girl turned out to be my "Topanga" For those of you unfamiliar with the TV show "Boy Meets World", I was Corey and she was Topanga. Our relationship was perfect and we talked and did everything best friends would do. Like Corey, I cared for her more and like Topanga she moved far away. The only difference to our stories is she never came back, never fell in love with me and our lives are spaced out. That same night I asked "Topanga" out, I remember running into my neighbor who was two years older than me. He wanted to know if I wanted to check out this new teen club in the area. Now at this time in my life, I didn't like dances but I wasn't feeling happy so I said Ok. That place ended up being a "drug" to me because now I was exposing myself to a multitude of women, most of who wanted the same thing I did. Through this place, I ended up meeting the first girl I ever said "I Love you to, and the first girl that "made me a man". Looking back, I don't regret anything I did because of that place but if I could go back, I would certainly do things much differently. I'll be the first to admit, my first time wasn't what it was all cracked up to be and wasn't special at all. It did however "drug" me and from that moment on, I was under the impression that all of what was going on was what I was supposed to do, you know drinking and driving, sex with random people and treating woman like objects instead of a people.

Guess who decided to come back around with flying colors to add fuel to the fire? You guessed it, my biologically mom. Take a wild guess where she moved too? Of all places she moved in right across the street from where I lived with my dad. Even though nearly ten years had passed since I had seen her, I still loved her but man, I had some resentment. Her living across from us was both a good and bad thing. The good was that we got to spend time with her but the bad thing was she was always drinking and most times incapacitated. I can't tell you how many times my brothers and I had to take care of her because she couldn't. I actually took her to the hospital one night when she was so drunk but it didn't seem out of ordinary until the doctor came out and told me her blood alcohol level was .31. I was so mad at her for allowing herself to get that way but what could I do, I was just 17 at the time. She was supposed to be the role model not the other way around. I began to think that it was ok to drink and get drunk, everyone was doing it so why not. And since my mom drank, she could buy it for me since I wasn't 21. Now because of this, other destructive doors were opened. During the rest of my high school life I said the heck with all of it. I was able to manipulate the school system and obtain the answer sheets to most of the tests I took and the ones I didn't I wrote the answers on my inner thigh or just guessed. I spent the vast amount of my time in Pottsville with different groups of people and didn't really see a future. Upon graduating and realizing these things, I began slowly fading away from all memories of my childhood but

some circumstances wouldn't let me.

CHAPTER 4

Finally there was relief in sight. I decided, with the pressures of my gram, to attend a small private college about an hour from where I lived. This gave me the opportunity to start over, be who I wanted to be and run from the past I so dearly hated. Do you know that you can't run from your problems? I just didn't know that at the time. Starting college, I was thrown into the fire immediately. All my anxieties were magnified but since these people didn't take the time to get to know me, I was never included in anything. I decided to go back to what I knew best and what made me happy and that was self-pleasuring and pornography. It got so bad that again it was almost a daily thing but who cares right? I even had a group of "friends" ask me to join them in a pizza and porn night which was highly uncomfortable at that stage in my life. For the first semester, I secluded myself from everyone and only came out to go to work and class. It was horrible. Then my life changed. I was sitting in my Food Safety class and three girls came up to me and invited me to their apartment to hang out and I accepted only because they were part of my major and everything seemed ok. Believe it or not though, that decision to let down the wall slightly opened up many more doors for me. My relationship with those three girls flourished but never exceeded anything but a friendship and I was ok with that. During this time, I was introduced to one of their friends from their hometown whom I really hit it off with. She was cute with a petite body but I didn't see a relationship forming just a good "casual friend". You see because of the damage done to me growing up all I really wanted from the girl was what everyone else was getting from her, a quick fix. The bad thing about it was I began to actually care about her and she took full advantage of it. Over the next few months, she would lead me on making me think she liked me when in actuality she was telling other guys the same thing. The bitterness and resentment to women was on the rise and I never stopped it. God did however provide a way out for me. I didn't know it at the time but I inherited something from my father, his work ethic. I gave 110% everyday to my job throughout my time at the private college. The semester before I was to graduate, both the general manager and assistant manager of where I worked pulled me into their office and sat me down to discuss my future. About twenty minutes into it, they suggested I apply to Penn State and obtain my bachelors in Hotel/Restaurant Management. I looked at them with a disappointment thinking "are you kidding me?" I cheated through high school and am barely making it through college, what makes you think Penn State will even look at me. All they asked from me was to apply so out of respect I did and guess what, I got in. That was the greatest thing that had ever happened to me up until that point and it certainly made me believe I can overcome anything. There were still demons inside of me that I was still running from so the acceptance to Penn State was very short-lived.

I went to my grams house after receiving the letter to talk to them. They were really proud of me but asked the question, "How is your relationship with God?" I honestly told them I had a relationship with him like most people did, you know church on holidays and talking to him only when I needed him. They kept at it and I was just listening to appease them, I just didn't want to hear it. Then my relationship with God went to hell later that night when I went to share the good news with my mentor, role model, friend and pastor. We were talking about things and I got on the subject of women. All he really cared to know was if I was sexually active but I paid it no mind because I didn't know what was going on at the time. He started feeding me double rum and cokes (which he knew were my favorite) and I began to slightly feel it. You know at 20, that's a great feeling so I kept at it. As I was leaving, I gave him a hug like I have done for the last nearly ten years and he proceeded to force himself on me and took me by the face and inserted his tongue in my mouth. I pulled away, turned around and walked out the door in complete and utter disgust. Driving home that night was such a surprise. All I could remember was thinking about was "Hey God, thanks for that, lets me know you care huh. All that stuff you say about loving your children, it's a lie and I want nothing to do with you ever!" Before I was to begin my time at Penn State, I was working a summer job at a local fast food restaurant where I met two awesome people who I would later realize would play a huge part in my confusion of woman. The first one was your wild and crazy, free spirited and very sexually opened. The other one was the complete opposite, shy and very reserved so it was like I was going for the best of both worlds. In the end I pursued the relationship with the quiet girl because at that time in my life that was what I was more attracted too. Now she knew I was going to Penn State so our relationship wasn't that serious until I came back for Thanksgiving break that year. I can remember showing up to her house and she was so nervous that I was flattered. That whole night her and her mom asked me a barrage of questions and then something amazing, yet unintentional happened. Her mom turned to her and said "Oh hey honey I forgot to give you the ring your gram had left for you". Tash then turned to me and asked me to put it on her finger and I wasn't paying much attention until I slipped it on her finger and that twinkle in her eyes made me realize what I had just done.

Over the next few weeks after I had gone back to college, we would keep in contact via text message and when I came home for Christmas that's when all the pieces to the puzzle came together. We literally hung out every day and during one of those days, she had invited me over to her sister's house for a little get together which I obviously accepted. That night, at this point of my life, was so magical I never had wanted it to end. She was so beautifully dressed in a pair of form fitting jeans and a blue cardigan that brought out all her features. I never had felt something like what I was feeling and well it took me off guard. We got to spent Christmas together but then I made the biggest mistake of our relationship. We had made plans to go to my cousin's house in Virginia for New Years and the day we were supposed to go we got into a huge argument over some really dumb stuff. When all was said and done, she didn't come with me. Before I left, I made her a promise that if anything was to ever happen that I'd be the first one there and last one to leave and as I left I gave her a huge hug so she at least knew I cared for her. Now I have this mindset that the way you ring in the New Year is exactly how your year will be. I texted her about 15 minutes before the ball was to drop and ask her if I could ring in the New Year with her and she said yes. In addition she sent me a text that I will never forget and it said "MAY THE SUN BE AT YOUR BACK AND WIND AT YOUR FEET". At the time I had no clue what that meant until I later learned that it was an Irish Blessing. As the clock neared midnight, I called her and she didn't answer. I continued to try throughout the night but she never answered so I was both mad and hurt that she did that to me. I came home from my cousins with the intention of giving her an ear full until I call her house and her grandfather answered. "Brian didn't you hear what happened?" In response I told him "No I haven't" and he told me to get the paper. I went to my closest friend's house and the second I picked up that paper, right on the front page was the news I didn't want to expect, Tasha was dead. I was devastated when I read that but luckily for me I was at a good friend's house. I couldn't believe what I had just seen and then it hit me. If we didn't have that disagreement, she would have been with me that night instead of in that car. Still to this date, I haven't been able to forgive myself for that. I know that God has a plan for everyone but I blame myself for messing up hers. She was so young and had so much potential but to lose her life so young, it hurts me. That's one of the reasons I don't like to argue with people, especially woman, because I don't want to be the cause of another's death you know. God showed me a blessing in all this though. I was asked by the family to be with them throughout the procession which was an extreme honor to me. The most significant aspect to all this was that after she was buried, all her family were given a single rose and her closest friends were given carnations, guess what I got? If you guessed a rose you'd be right on. I believe that was the first time I ever felt a part of something but look at what it cost me? You know what I did though, I kept to my promise. All though I couldn't be there at first, I was the last person to leave that gravesite that day because a promise to me is a promise no matter what the circumstances. For the longest time, I kept the situation with Tasha and my pastor bottled up inside and took it with me to back to Penn State where I let it fester until I lost it.

Chapter 5

I spent all three years in the party scene. I would start on Tuesday and only rest on Sunday. I valued relationships with guys but didn't care for any relationship with woman. During my tenure, however, there were one really special women that crossed my path and looking back had saved me from complete destruction. I was 23 when I met my first love, Avrah. She was so smart, absolutely gorgeous with her long brown hair and dark eyes, and surprisingly who cared about me for me and all my quirks and downfalls. We had a great relationship but again I never fixed my past so when things came to light, I was completely destroyed. In addition, I didn't think I was ever good enough for her. One time, and I know it seems small, but we were coming back from Spring Break and her dad took us out to dinner but beforehand we went to the grocery store. While at the store I wanted a soda and candy bar and he told me that he'd pay for it and I told him that I got it so in turn he paid for it and told me that money wasn't anything to him. I felt horrible about it because I thought he did it because he didn't think I could take care of his girl. On top of that, since I had been cheated on countless times and was always the back up, I assumed she was doing the same thing. Before I could get hurt I found me a backup who was feeding me all I needed to hear. I eventually broke up with Avrah and pursued this other girl thinking things were good but I learned that it was all a game. Not only did she leave me hanging but I lost the first and only girl who truly ever loved me and I snapped. Coming back that following fall semester Avrah had sent me a letter that just until I started writing this book did I realize how much she really loved me. Here you be the judge:

From: "Avrah"

To: "Brian"

Date: Sunday, August 07, 2005 6:15 PM

Hey.. um..

So I just wanted to tell you that I'm sorry about everything.

From being angry at you both lately and all of last

semester to hurting you with stuff that I've done to

everything else. I still don't think I did anything wrong

in the past few weeks, but I do care that I hurt you. But you

probably don't really believe me, but I'll tell you anyways.

I care about you and love you, no matter what you or I do.

I just can't believe it turned out like this is all. We've

known each other for almost a year now and I still

feel like we really don't get the other one. We may hear

each other's sides, but we're both two stubborn to actually

change how we feel even if we have intentions of it.

Because we'll think about it, and then just decide we

were right. I think that was probably a big problem of

ours. But what I think I don't understand is why you just

gave up. I don't get why you stopped wanting to try to work

it out with me. And I remember a long time ago you said

how you would never break up with me, unless I cheated on

you. And that turned out to be so untrue, I'd be mad about

it, but I didn't believe you when you said it anyways.

But I had a conversation with someone about some stuff the

other day. And do you think that the reason you feel like I

don't care about you because of what I did with Mark and

Jason was because you couldn't hook up with whoever

those girls were. And you feel like if I felt the same towards

you as you felt towards me, I should be acting the same as

you? Think about that and if you think that is how you feel,

you should know by now how different we are. And that I

can still care about you and love you and have done

that. Even if that's not something you could do. What I wasn't sure of that made it okay in my mind to do that was if we should be together, but it didn't mean that I didn't love you and care about you like nuts Brian. Maybe think about that okay? Maybe you'll understand where I'm coming from better. Because it really hurts me when you tell me you think I don't care about you. And I react by getting pissed, not the best way to handle it I'm sure but, hey I haven't really been handling much of anything really well lately. I love you and want to be friends with you, but I'm scared that we're not going to be able to do it. I mean can you seriously say that you can be around me and not have a problem with me or want to hold me or hate me or love me or whatever? Because I'm not sure that I can. I can't imagine spending time with you and not being with you. Maybe in time, I dunno. I think that's all I have to say for the moment.

"Avrah"

Looking back on this I still couldn't understand that someone actually loved me. I didn't truly absorb this letter until recently and I feel so bad. All the problems I had with women growing up and not handling them according to God, I ended up losing a great girl. I tried ever so hard to win her love back but the devil wasn't having it. The first week back at school Avrah called me crying asking me if she could come get me so we can talk. Of course I accepted because I still loved her but she wouldn't tell me what was wrong and I was worried. When she arrived, she was in the worst condition I had ever seen her in. After she told me what happened to her that weekend, I was devastated but still tried to hold my composure and be there for her. She had asked me to come back to her apartment for dinner and a movie so I accepted not having any idea that my life was about to get blown apart. After dinner, we went to her room and were watching a movie and she wanted to be held and I didn't second guess it. Not even five minutes later my hand was placed in an inappropriate place and I quickly pulled away and said "This wasn't going to happen" Guess what she said afterward, "Brian I think you better leave". I walked home that night and cried my eyes out wondering what the heck just happened. For the rest of the semester, I crashed. I was failing all my classes, got fired from my job and was drunk almost every day.

I started thinking that life's not worth it anymore and wanted to take my life. Before I had made this decision, I consulted a friend and she loved me so much she wouldn't leave my side. She had me stay with her until she felt comfortable even if that meant her missing classes or band practice. She was a real hero! My sadness though, because I didn't deal with it immediately, escaladed to anger and betrayal. Instead of moving on with my life, I started texting and calling and showing up to Avrah apartment pretty frequently. People were telling me left and right what she was doing and it was destroying her and I couldn't handle not being there for her. It got so bad she called the cops and got a restraining order against me which then turned my anger to deep depression. I was never in trouble in my life until that moment and I couldn't handle it. This time I said the wrong thing to the right person and they called the cops who in turn came to get me and took me away to a psychiatric hospital. My life was in complete ruins! During my stint in the hospital, I really learned a lot about myself and not allowing the past to dictate my future. One of the hardest thing I had to deal with and dealt with up until just about two years ago was that when I was in this hospital my dad told me he couldn't come see me because he was busy working. I was so hurt because I had nearly lost my life and at this really low time for me I'd expect my dad of all people to be there. My mom did come and I am grateful but she didn't have to, my dad should have been there. Like every other time in my life, I just had to brush it off and get over it! I did returned back to Penn

State with an open-mind and a new outlook on life. Regrettably I still had an immense hatred toward the female gender so I began a new trend, hit and run (having sex then running away). Where was God during all this? All my close friends had graduated and the two I had left, one was involved in a relationship with Avrah's closest friend and the other one really didn't do much with himself as far as the social scene was concerned. This made matters even more dangerous for me because now I could do whatever I wanted and not have to explain myself. I attended a few parties and still stayed pretty active in the nightlife and although anger could never bring me to stooping so low as to commit a hit and run, I did have a lot of meaningless flings. Guess who I had run into during this phase? Remember that girl Shelia from high school that I use to work with, well she was now attending the same school and completely blew me off like I never existed. After I seen her something inside me kicked on. As much as I wanted to "hit and run", the rest of the night was just a damper. Shelia made me realize subconsciously that I still had some type of respect for woman. Also in the back of my mind, I would be thinking "What would my gram and Sister Edna think of my behavior". The problem with this is "what about my parents". Never, during my whole tenure at Penn State, did they actually know how I was doing until it was too late. June 5th, 2006 was a day that I will never forget. I was lying in my bed studying for one of my hospitality classes when my phone rang. "Mr. Donnelly this is the Grangeville Hospital and we regret to inform you but you mother has passed away this morning and she listed you as her contact". What in the world had just happened? Where did this come from? What was I supposed to do? I was never really close to my biological mom but at this moment I felt like my world just came crashing down. My mom never had or seemed like she wanted anything to do with me or my brothers and now she's gone for good and I'll never know why we weren't good enough. How can a mom do this to her sons? The questions began filling my head before, during and after the funeral and now they will never be answered and I didn't like it. First the incident with Avrah, then my mom, what else was there? I had nothing. My birth mom was gone, no girlfriend, my grades weren't good and my parents ceased to exist but I did have one thing, my work ethic. Because of that ethic, I was given hope; a shot at a great job in North Carolina. Bingo a new start, no one knows me and I can do whatever and be whoever I wanted to be...AGAIN!

CHAPTER 6

My decision to move to North Carolina and accept this amazing job didn't actually turn out the way I dreamed. For the first year I was there, I did very well as a manager but I failed as a person. You know I was a northern boy in a southern world and women ate it up. My ability to gain the trust of women came so easily. That first year was destructive. for me both mentally and physically. I continued the trend from college by partying every night but this time, I was able to manipulate women into thinking I actually cared which made it so much easier to commit the hit and run. My life was in a downward spiral and in self destruction mode. Eventually, because of my decisions with a woman, I lost my great job. What makes matters worse is that I did what was right with this girl but after she realized she didn't have control of me anymore she called me crying, telling me she was pregnant which I later discovered to be a lie. She only did this because she had lost the control and realized she was wrong but needed a reason to get the attention off her and back on me and it worked. You know God still did make an effort to be an important part of my life but I was so destroyed at the time I didn't even realize it. God sent a guardian angel to me when I needed one the most. He sent an older woman who was ironically from the same area in Pennsylvania as I was. After a few weeks knowing this lady we became roommates. If she hadn't provided me a room, I would probably still be living on the streets as we speak. I went from a good paycheck to now working for minimum wage and trying to make ends meet. You would have thought I would have gotten smarter and got my life straight? Of course that didn't stop me from partying and having fun, I just had to be a little bit smarter about it now. For the next three years, I went through seven jobs, four living situations and I can't even began to count the number of women that came and went. I knew something had to change, and fast.

One day I decided to call my father and ask him if I could move into the house he was not using for a little bit just to get back on my feet. In October of 2010, I packed up my stuff and put my life in NC on hold not having the faintest idea of what was going to be there when I returned. Over the next four months, I did what I knew best and that was work. Almost everyday, I worked two jobs, 5am until 2pm then to the other job from 5pm until 10. In my free time, I was with my gram and Sister Edna trying to re-establish the relationship I had lost with God over the years. Both of them helped me learn a lot about who God is and what his purpose is for me. During this time I met a beautiful young lady from the area and we instantly hit it off. This relationship though wasn't really a relationship. We hung out a lot but there was absolutely no love what so ever. You see my relationship with God was actually improving but since I was weak I submitted to my sinful desires. This young lady and I were sexually active with no strings attached. After a night of partying, the truth about her came out. The guy that she told me was her landlord ended up being another no strings attached relationship. The most disgusting part of it all was that but he was nearly twice her age but had a lot of money. I was devastated, not because she wasn't my girlfriend but because I was slowly letting my guard down and look at what had transpired. The worst part of all this was a few months later I found out she was pregnant and the time of conception was around the time we had last bonded. I did my best to see what was going on but because this guy has a lot more money than I did and through some prayer I decided that I didn't want to ruin a child's life in a broken home. Now grant it, I may not be the father, but my heart really tells me that I am. I just believe he is in better hands either way. Even through all this, I turned to God and asked why? Weren't things supposed to get better before they got worse? Little did I know God had a miracle waiting for me back in North Carolina, I just wasn't quite ready for it yet. You know I was at my grams a few days before Christmas talking about things and trying to understand why God was doing this to me and she brought out her bible to show me what God was saying. "Here look Brian, in Matthew Ch 25:21 it says *'You have been faithful in handling the little stuff so now I will give you many more responsibilities.'*" What in the world was he talking about? I haven't done well at all throughout my life. What was I about embark on? And this new challenge was I really ready? Over the next two months, I lived nervously wondering what in the world was happening to me. I went back to North Carolina for a quick visit during the second week of January to celebrate a good friend's birthday but like the girl in Pennsylvania, I willingly participated in activities that I now am sorry for. I was under the impression we were just celebrating her birthday and it led to a night of wild drunk sexual bliss which in most cases would have been great but she was also married and I just didn't care. Like many of the other women who came before her, I wanted what I wanted and didn't care of the repercussions.

The day was January 17th, 2011, I remember as if it was yesterday. The snow was falling heavily and the temperature was dropping fast. Everything was shut down, not a single vehicle on the road; it truly was a state of emergency. I was letting my dog out when I received a text message from my best friend in North Carolina. It read "Hey Brian, I have got this great girl I'd like to introduce you to. I think you'd be perfect for her, you want her number?" Now I had known my best friend for almost four years and we had always talked and shared everything. She knew exactly what I liked in a woman but also knew I wasn't one to quickly jump into anything so I ended up taking the number and giving it a shot….what did I have to lose? Later that evening, I sent a message to her introducing myself and then a conversation ensued. That night still brings a smile to my face just because of the time I was able to spend with her. I can't explain it but she made me feel so comfortable. To ease the curiosity, she sent me a picture of herself and let me tell you what, was I blown away. She was sitting in her car with a purple vest on, her hair all done up and a smile that would bring a light to any dark room. She didn't even have make up on and to other people would have looked like a mess but to me this is when I feel a woman looks her best. My goodness, it still amazes me how someone could be so beautiful. Now I was very cautious about this though. Like most woman I had met up until that time, we had just talked about sex, nothing more or less, but not her. We talked nearly every day for two months, at least three hours a day and maybe a handful of times did the conversation wandered but it never got out of hand. Two months into us talking, we decided that I was ready to move back and start my new life in NC with her and her kids. Before I had officially moved in, she was sending me little love notes through the mail, birthday and Valentines Day cards and the key to her apartment with a note saying "this is the key to our future". I understand this might have seemed like we were moving fast but something in my heart was telling me "Wake up Brian" and I was tired of ignoring it.

CHAPTER 7

My best friend sent me an invitation to her son's birthday party in the first week of March and this was my perfect chance to surprise her and take that leap of faith that I so dreaded. Bailey knew I wasn't quite ready or prepared to come back to NC for financial reasons at that time but this surprise trip was well prepared for. I embarked for the journey to NC two nights before I was scheduled to be there so I could surprise her. All the way down I spoke to her and she never even knew it. All I could think about on the way down was that I was going to be there to hold her that night. It was hilarious though because throughout the conversation she kept saying "Oh I wish you were here to hold me" and I kept saying, soon sweetie soon, but she didn't catch it which was absolutely amazing! The weather for the trip down to NC couldn't be any better. The sky was filled with stars, the air crisp and hardly any traffic whatsoever, God knew what he was doing. I arrived at my destination shortly after midnight and with my key in hand, opened the door quietly and seen my sleeping beauty laying on the couch. She looked so amazing I wish I could have captured that moment but I certainly did in my heart. Her hair was an absolute mess, no make-up on and in sweats, the perfect combination. At first she was startled until she realized it was me and that smile she had began to illuminate the room like the stars were doing outside. She didn't realize it but I guess when she is either sleepy or really happy her lips quiver which on her looks absolutely sexy.

The feelings were incredible, the passion was certainly there, and having her in my arms at that moment, there isn't a word that can explain that. As we laid there looking into each other's eyes, my heart was starting to flutter, my breathe increasing but my past started rearing its ugly head. We both made what would be the beginning of a lot of dumb spiritual decisions based on our past and agreed to make love that night. Now don't get me wrong, it was consenting and absolutely amazing but if I could go back truthfully I wouldn't have partake in it. First thing the next morning, I was awakened by two of the most precious little children that could only have been a blessing from God. As I laid there, Bailey proceeded to explain to Blake and Brooke that I was mommy's new friend. I was taken away at how beautiful Bailey was at being a mommy. Don't tell her but at that single moment, I knew she was the one and that a future was certainly in the making. When she left to take the young-ins (yes Southern life is rubbing off on me) to daycare, I looked at the ceiling and started to get really scared. I began asking myself "What did I do to deserve her?" and began doubting that I was even good enough. All day long I unfortunately slept because I was afraid to face my fears of rejections but then around 2pm I received an unexpected visit. Bailey came back to the apartment on her lunch break and we just laid there in complete silence. Her smell and soft touch eased my uncertainty I may have been feeling. Man after the kids and Bailey had got home later that afternoon, my anxiety was at full throttle but just like earlier in the day, Baileys presences eased any uncomfortableness I was feeling. Do you know how great of a feeling it is to have two children welcome you like they've known you all their lives? After the kids went to bed, Bailey and I were sitting on the couch watching tv when she turned to me and told me "Brian we are going to breakfast tomorrow morning with my family. They really want to meet you". I looked at her and calmly agreed but boy deep down inside my anxiety sky rocketed. I enjoy meeting new people but meeting parents is a really big move and only after one day, I was intimidated.

The next morning as we pulled up to the restaurant, I looked at her with fright, "Bailey, I don't know if I can do this". Looking me dead in the eyes, I suddenly forgot any anxiety I was feeling. "Everything will be ok, baby. My parents are really nice. They'll love you". Ok Bailey I believe you, lets do this. Opening the door for Bailey and the kids, I see this really petite middle aged woman smiling radiantly and I knew this had to be her mom. Hey Brian, these are my parents Randy and Annie. "Pleasure to meet you guys" as I extend my right hand to greet Randy but as I did the same thing to Annie, she pulled me in for a hug. "Sweetie we don't shake hands here, we hug". Being completely caught off guard, I followed her family into the restaurant and took my seat between Bailey and her mom, anxiety actually at a standstill. All I can think of was "Brian just don't talk and you won't mess up". Halfway into breakfast, Annie began the barge of questions but surprisingly I wasn't fazed. For reasons I will never understand it was so much easier talking to her family then anyone I ever had before but also playing in the back of my mind I kept wondering why Bailey was truly into me? So Brian, what's your religious background Annie stated?

Well I grew up Catholic but my relationship with God isn't strong at all just because I have a bad taste in my mouth. Really...what's happened? I'm sorry I just don't want to talk about it right now. I'm sorry. That's ok sweetie, I understand. If you ever want to talk, I'm listening. God loves you though, just don't forget it, ok. Leaving the restaurant that day I was beginning to feel something inside of me that I had never felt, somewhat of a tug but I paid absolutely no attention to it. So what did you think of my family asked Bailey? Truthfully, your mom is so amazing but your dad, well he seemed slightly standoffish. He didn't really say much and I wasn't sure what to say to him. That's ok Brian, I'm a daddy's girl. He was just being protective. I understand its ok I have nothing to hide. I have dated my fair share of woman in my life and met some astonishing families but walking out of that restaurant that day I began feeling something funny. For the rest of that weekend, Bailey and I had shared some remarkable conversations about our lives and what we wanted the future to be. One night while laying in bed, I seen her shirt was raised a little and her sexiest feature was exposed, her "tiger stripes". While her whole body was perfect, and besides her butt, I absolutely love her stomache and those tiger stripes. I use to think they were a deterrent until I realized what they meant. Before I left to go back to PA, we agreed on one thing, that we were going to start our lives together. I remember leaving for PA that Sunday afternoon because I had a few things to tighten up before I moved back. As I was pulling away, I seen Bailey, in my Penn State hoodie, tearing up and it really touched me in ways words couldn't describe. Over the next two weeks, the bond between us was growing stronger and stronger and I couldn't even begin to count the days until we would be together.

Chapter 8

As I arrived back in NC for good, my life as a bachelor was over and my new role as a step daddy begun. Unfortunately, my heart was ready but my mind wasn't and that didn't make for a good combination. Bailey's kids were so precious and so young I didn't know what to do, so I just panicked. I "hid" in my job and working out, leaving Bailey to do all the work with the children as well as the house work too. Man I tell you, do I regret that even to this day. No woman should ever have to bear the burden of a household and children while the man enjoys life. It doesn't matter if you're dating, engaged or married, the relationship should be fair and just. What made matters even worse is that we both "hid" behind being a parents and wanted to live freely, going out to the clubs and drinking every weekend. For our relationship, that wrong foot we got off on in the beginning, continued when we lived together. One night I was laying on the couch and Bailey came in and woke me up. "Brian I'm not happy anymore, me and the kids are going to my mom's for a few days". You see I'm very good at reading people and I knew something was not right and that wasn't the issue. After she had left, I called her mom because we had that kind of relationship to ask for advice. During the conversation, I asked if Bailey was staying there like she said and her mom had no idea what I was talking about. You know the first thing that popped in my head was that she was cheating on me. I drove around that day with my heart racing wondering what I did or why wasn't I good enough? My only option at this moment was to go to my best friend's house, you know the same one who got me and Bailey together, and talk. Well as I arrived, I saw Bailey pulling up and waited until she finished parking. With my heart pounding, I got out of my car and she noticed me and her jaw dropped. "Bailey what are you doing here, I thought you were sleeping at your mom's?" After I confronted her she said nothing and as I watched her go to my friend's house with the kids, Lyle, my friend's brother and Bailey's obsession, came outside and I knew then what was really going on. Regretfully, I will admit, I lost my cool as I smashed her keys off the ground in fury and got in my car and left. I don't remember how I made it home that day but I did. Throughout the rest of that night, I laid in bed, tossing and turning, wondering why and now what? Where I was I going to go? What was I going to do? Around 1:30am that night, I received a text message from Bailey asking me if it was ok for her to come back to the house and without thinking I said "Yes". When she got home and put the kids to bed, she came into the room crying. "Brian I'm so sorry, she stated. Can I come lay down with you?" At this point in the night, I wasn't quite sure how I was feeling so without thinking I said yes again. Holding her in my arms, the warmth of her skin on mine and her head gently resting on my chest, for some reason made all the pain disappear and I forgot why I was hurting.

While holding her she admitted that she slept with Lyle but said that all they did was kiss and I gave her the benefit of the doubt because everyone deserves a chance. I was questioning in my head that if all it was a kiss then why did she feel so bad?

Unfortunately at this moment in my life, I was in the business of getting even, so I figured that I was entitled to cheat as well. A few weeks later, I did the same thing to her because I thought it was ok. Lesson for all you who are reading this…it doesn't make things even I promise. For the next few months, our relationship was an extremely fast rollercoaster ride with a lot of ups and certainly a lot of downs but I was buckled in. I was slowly learning that God was driving though. One of the most unusual things throughout this ride was the love being shown from her family but especially her mother. One of her mother's strongest characteristics was her love for God and sharing him with everyone. You see my relationship with God was just an "I'll see you on Sunday and when I need you" kind of relationship. I didn't truly know who he was or what anything truly meant. Bailey's family was very adamant on going to church every Sunday and just to appease them I went but slept most of the time. For the first year of our relationship, I didn't really care to have any such relationship with God because like growing up where was he for me when I needed him? During all this, and without my knowledge, her parents were praying for God to come into my life and break down the walls I had for him. I never was in a situation where someone cared enough for me enough to pray so hard for God to influence. Yes, growing up I had my gram and her friend to pray for me but I didn't really get anything from it because they are family and I assumed that it was just because I was I family. They did influence me tremendously and God did do work through me but again I didn't have a strong foundation and had no idea what was going on. You know I look back and realized that because of my gram and her friend, I met Bailey's parents who in my opinion and belief were the ones who took over for them when I moved back to NC. At times, I felt so awkward because of the presence of God that I began shutting myself off to Bailey, the kids and her family. I then decided to go back to my default where I started working longer hours and spending more time at the gym. For me, there was always an excuse not a solution. The devil saw this and started to exploit all of my weaknesses and I couldn't control them. First, he began to fill my head with thoughts of "Brian you don't really need her, I could provide for you everything you need and want. We can just keep her around until you get bored and have her as a fall back. She has kids too so if you don't listen to me all the fun you want would be done for. Is that what you want?" Man those words coming from him at this moment in my life felt so good. I kept thinking back to being rejected as a youth and then my situation in college and to top it off what Bailey did, or didn't do, that night with Lyle. It wasn't rocket science, this was what I wanted and who cares who I'd hurt along the way. The devil decided to bring back a woman from my past that I had felt strongly for but never pursued it because it just didn't feel right. Well, for about a month, I was secretly texting her and she was sending me naked pictures enticing me that I can have her anytime I wanted. She decided to show up to my work and not even five minutes later Bailey showed up as well. My heart was racing and I frankly didn't know what to do but Bailey didn't know who she was. If my relationship with God was like it is now I would have realized this was his way of convicting me. Later that night, when everyone was gone and I was closing up, this girl and I went into the bathroom and frankly did a "hit and run". She knew I was in a relationship and wanted to do this. I wanted to get what I want and make her pay as well. Well little did I know but I felt absolutely horrible afterwards. Even though I just did what I did, it actually shattered that wall I had around my heart of anger and hatred and lust I had bottled up. When I got home that night, I laid next to Bailey and felt such shame and regret that I couldn't hold her or even talk to her and when she asked I just played it off as I had a really bad night. Now you would think the devil had done what he had done so he would be finished, well you're wrong.

Over the next few weeks, I couldn't be the man Bailey deserved so I had succumbed to satisfying my desires with pornography. I kept thinking to myself I'm not good enough and that Bailey was so beautiful so why me so something fake was a better solution, at least I couldn't fail there. Meanwhile, I also had to put on a fake persona that everything was ok so I didn't have to face reality. I worked and worked so much that roughly in a given week, I'd see Bailey and the kid's maybe a day total. My life and relationship was slowly deteriorating and I was on a down whirl spiral to hell until I got an unexpected wake up call. I was out to my normal bi-weekly lunch with Bailey's mom when the conversation we were having knocked me right out. "Brian sweetie what's wrong? Lately you have been so distant that it's really upsetting Bailey and rubbing off on the kids? You know you're family and you can tell me anything right? A deafening silence came over the table that for a moment I was speechless. All of a sudden, I broke down and began to cry. "Mom, I'm so sorry I'm so sorry. I had sex with another woman and I feel absolutely terrible about it. Then to make matters worse, I hid behind work and pornography and completely shut myself off to your daughter and those kids. I love them so much but I don't deserve them at all for what I did and I'll understand if you're upset with me. "Son, I really don't know what to say. I'm not mad or upset, just disappointed. I know you love my daughter and those kids but I also know Satan is attacking you but you have got to be stronger than he is." "But mom, I don't know what to do." "Don't worry Brian, I have been praying and will continue to pray for you that God works in your life and you got to let him" "I know mom but I made a mistake and I don't want to lose Bailey or those kids, they are my world". "I know they are but you need to tell the truth. I can't guarantee you what will happen but I will pray for God to deliver you from this struggle. Please remember I will always love you, and you will always be considered a part our family, I love you son". Man I can remember looking into her dark eyes that day and seeing something I don't think I had ever truly seen, a genuine, sincere look that actually had me believe that someone really did care. Later that evening after the kids were in bed, I laid silently in bed, Bailey's head on my chest, both of us in complete silence. My heart began to race and Bailey turned to me with a worried concern, "Baby what's wrong, and are you ok?" Bailey we need to talk. I have to get something of my chest or I'm going to lose it". Taking Bailey by the hand I looked her straight in the eyes and let it all out. "I'm so sorry but I had sex with another woman a few weeks ago and I regret it more than you can imagine". Suddenly tears began streaming from Baileys eyes and in an instant she slipped away from my grasp and turned her back to me as she laid there sobbing. "Please Bailey forgive me I'm so sorry" "How could you Brian, what did I ever do to you?" I'll be honest. When you were with Lyle that hurt me so much I thought it would be ok to even the score, you know you did so why can't I?" In an instant Bailey turns around, the tears stopped and are replaced with a deafening silence. "You know what Brian, you hurt me but I love you and forgive you and I understand why you did this. Let's both drop this and pretend neither of these situations ever happened and start over?" I'm ok with that but again I'm really sorry I never wanted to hurt you but you crushed me and I was on the defense, still no excuse but yes its done, never to be brought up again.

Later that night while Bailey and the kids were sleeping I did something I never did in my entire life. I went out on the back deck and looked up into the crisp, clear sky and had one of my many heart-to-heart conversations with God. Looking up to the sky, I began to ponder what was going on here. I was getting so furious at myself and God because I couldn't figure out what I was supposed to do. "God what the heck are you doing? What am I supposed to do? Annie tells me you love me and want what's best for me, well is this it? And if so what the heck is going on?" Truthfully I'm sure at this moment God was answering my questions but I was so enraged that even if he was, I wasn't paying any attention. Days turn into weeks and weeks into months and suddenly out of nowhere I felt a huge weight being lifted off my chest, I started falling in love with this girl but I panicked and ran to my security blanket, her mom. "Mom, I really need to talk to you. Something is going on and I have no idea what it means

and it's scaring me". "Talk to me honey what's wrong".
"I'm falling in love with your daughter and I've already
fallen in love with them kids but is that ok, am I allowed
to?' With a slight giggle Annie responded, "Yes honey its
ok to feel this way, have you told Bailey yet?" "No mom I
haven't I'm so scared that it will scare her away. I don't
want to risk it or risk being hurt". "Don't worry sweetie be
honest you'll be ok". On the way back to our house, I was
channel surfing and came across *K-Love*, a well-known
Christian radio station and the song that was playing gave
me the necessary sign I needed to confirm that I really was
falling in love with her. I blasted *"Love Never Fails" by
Jesus Culture* all while trying to maintain a level of
calmness. I opened the door that night and saw Bailey and
the kids all nestled up on the couch watching cartoons. All
of a sudden, the kids came barreling towards me with their
arms stretched out and the both of them almost knocked me
over. The oldest gave me a bear hug and our little princess

gave me a peck on the cheek that melted my heart. "I love you guys". Bailey, sweetie I have some good news for you but I'll tell you when the kids go to bed, right now I just want to sit with you all and watch some cartoons. While sitting there with them, their eyes glued to the TV I looked up and without hesitation spoke in a soft monotone to God, "Thank you". Later that evening after the kids we tucked away soundly, Bailey turns gracefully to me and with a glowing smile blurts out, "Baby I can't wait anymore what's this good news you have for me". "Ok you might need to sit down for this not realizing we were already laying in the bed but that's ok. So over the last few months you have been nothing less than my rock. You know you don't know it but sometimes I wake up before you and just watch you sleep. You are absolutely beautiful and I think it's about time you should know something about me. I know that without a doubt that, and a slight pause took over, Bailey Ashley, I Love You with all my heart. I love those kids but did I mention I love you even more. I know I haven't been the best person to deal with but you believe in me and I believe in you and in us. I don't know what the future holds, all I know is that I want you to be with me for the ride.

I can't even begin to express how I felt at that moment in my life. Something was going on, changes were happening but I couldn't explain them for the life of me. Although I was in love there was something deeper inside of me that wasn't allowing me to be happy. What was it? What was missing? You know what was missing, God. During my whole relationship, the one thing that was stressful was to have that relationship with God but I simply wasn't having it. I would go to church with Bailey and her family but wouldn't really grasp any messages that were being preached about. Again, my past experiences with the church really left a bad taste in my mouth that I wasn't willing to endure it again. Of course God wasn't having that and neither were her parents. Little did I know but behind the scenes Annie and the rest of her family were aggressively praying for me to realize that God loves me. The devil wasn't at all ready to let me go so he turned up the heat and life became a pile of mass confusion. The sexual temptations were coming at me faster than I have ever experienced in my entire life. I had no clue what to do about it but just enjoy the ride and not care what happened or who I hurt. Now my strength in Christ was certainly getting stronger but the devil knew what to do to confuse me and put me into a bad place. I was sitting at work texting my best friend, you know the same girl who got me and Bailey together, and apparently she and Bailey had a falling out that I didn't know about. I was trying to make the situation better when all of a sudden she asked me my opinion on something involving her boyfriend that was out of town. She sent me a pornographic picture depicting a bondage situation and it suddenly had my thoughts racing.

She invited me over to her apartment for a little bit just to hangout and talk about rekindling hers and Bailey's friendship. When I got there, she was half drunk and being really flirty but I paid no mind to it initially though. As I sat there, I could feel the devil tugging at my heart and whispering in my ear "Brian, she won't tell, you know you have wanted to do this since you first met her, now here is your shot, go for it". Now you see the problem wasn't that it was there, the problem was I loved Bailey and didn't want to hurt her but regretfully I still had pent up hurt for her sleeping with this girl's brother so I said "Screw it". The best part of it all, even though I messed up, was that in the middle of the rendezvous all I could think about was Bailey. I don't think I would have been able to do anything if Bailey wasn't on my mind. I know that's still no explanation but to me it was worth mentioning. When I left the apartment that night, I made a very conscious decision to separate myself from this girl, not only because of what had happened, but I also realized that she wasn't the person I met when I first moved her. The devil knew to use her and I fell for it. On the way home that night and not even understanding what I was doing, I asked God for his forgiveness and I vowed to never do anything like that again. God did answer me that night but my goodness I was afraid and didn't fully listen to him and that turned out to be the biggest mistake of my life. You think I told Bailey about this? Unfortunately, I did not and assumed I could sweep it under the rug, you know what she don't know won't hurt her now will it? I believed that I got what I wanted without having to pay the price. As each day past, my conscience weighed heavily and it took a toll on me but I wasn't going to allow it to destroy me or my relationship this time. I began praying harder and harder for my relationship and I even became more involved in our church. Bailey and I, as one, began to take classes to better our relationship from financial to parenting. We weren't

going to allow our past to dictate our future.

Chapter 9

January 29th, 2012, the day that changed both of our lives both physically and spiritually. I was sitting in church with Bailey and her family and the presence of God hit me like a ton of bricks. The choir began to sing the same song I heard the night I told Bailey that I loved her and while the song was being sung, we both simultaneously turned to each and I knew it at that moment I wanted this girl to be my wife. "Baby, are you ok? Your face looks flushed" Bailey asked. "Yes I feel great. God is good. I love you and I'm so lucky your mine". I looked over at her mom and she knew it and all she did was smile. After we got home that night, I went out to the back deck and just gazed into the sky with a huge smile on my face. The next day I knew the decision I was about to make was exactly what I was destined to do. I sent both her parents a text message telling them I really needed to talk to the both of them and that this was very important to me but Bailey couldn't know a thing.

"Brian have a seat what's wrong, is everything ok? After we got the text we both started praying for you hoping that you're ok" You know her mom always worried about me and the little things like that let me know that what I was doing was right. "Mom and dad, I have been doing a lot of praying and meditating and God has clearly spoken to me. I called you here today to ask your permission to marry your daughter. I have never loved someone the way that I love her. She really brings out the best in me and I want that for the rest of my life." The room got very quiet and a long pause ensued then her father spoke up "Are you serious Brian, do you think you can take care of my daughter and those kids and give them a happy life?" "Sir the only thing I can guarantee you is that I will do my best. Like I said before I love her with all my heart and want to spend the rest of my life with her, grow with her and die with her, I just need your permission" "Then Brian you have our blessing. Just promise us you won't hurt her" An overwhelming sensation overcame me that I had to sit down. My heart was pounding, my palms were sweating but boy was I smiling ear to ear. "So when are you going ask her?" "I plan to ask her tomorrow night at dinner. Can you watch the kids for us that night? I will have everything ready for you that all you need to do is give them baths?" "Yes son we certainly will and we know she's going to be happy" as her parents both embraced me tightly and saw me out the door.

You know after I left their house that afternoon, I really can't remember a single thing I did except for when I picked up the ring. The thought of marriage and all it brought was scaring the living daylights out me. I kept asking myself am I good enough for her? It's so funny because all my life I thought about this day, planning how I would do it and now the time was here and frankly it terrified me. The next night after we dropped the kids off and arrive at dinner, I couldn't help but realize how in the world I got a girl like her. She was wearing a pair of ever so form fitting jeans and I believe a light blue shirt (I could be wrong but that's what my heart is telling me). She looked absolutely radiant walking into the restaurant that evening and I knew what I was about to do was what I was meant to do. Dinner was absolutely delicious but I couldn't concentrate on anything. I completely forgot how I was going to ask her and the ring was in my pocket so I couldn't do anything without her picking up on things. Luckily for me, she was a typical woman and got up saying "Hey I'm going to freshen up I'll be right back". Bingo here was my opportunity to seize the moment. The waiter came over to drop the check off and I told him what I was about to do and that as long as the check was still standing on the table he was not to come back. When Bailey arrived back at the table, I had the ring sitting on the seat out of view and told her "we need to talk about us". "Is everything ok, Brian? Something seems weird." Taking her by the hand, I looked her dead in the eye and said "you know we have been together for a while but I really don't know how you feel about me". You see this was my subconscious attempt to see where her feelings were at because I was so scared of being rejected and I couldn't fathom her saying no. "Brian sweetie, you know how much I love you. You are an absolutely amazing man who treats me great and loves my kids like his own. I have never met someone like you before. My whole family absolutely adores you and the fact that you love them as much as you do lets me know you're for real. Where is all this coming from? What about you, how do you feel" "Bailey I really don't know how to tell you this. You are such an amazing woman and did I ever tell you how absolutely gorgeous you are? Sometimes I wonder why you're even wasting your time with me. You know I'm so proud of you for overcoming what life has thrown at you. And then to see all you have achieved in this short time we have been together makes me believe you're going to do big things. You get so self-conscious about when I rub your stomach but I do that because I secretly can't wait and hope one day we can have a baby even though I know you can't. Bailey, I have been doing a lot of thinking about us and I unfortunately got something to tell you. I don't want to be your boyfriend anymore I am so sorry, and then with a quick swipe of the ring from the chair, I want to be your husband so Bailey "Will you marry me?" "Brian are you serious as tears began spilling from her eyes" "I have never been more sure of anything in my life" "Of course I will" as both of us met in the center of the table and locked lips for the first time as an engaged couple "Hey everyone she said yes!" All of a sudden a huge uproar erupted and the entire restaurant began clapping as we both stood up and embraced each other tightly. You know as loud as the restaurant was that night the only thing I can could hear was Bailey telling me she loved me. You know how you always hear people say that sometimes they feel like they are floating on a cloud, well I can attest to that same feeling. On the way home that night, we decided to take the long way home but she insisted on calling nearly every contact in her phone. You know in all the time I had known her, this was the happiest I had ever seen her and I was really glad I could be a part of it. Arriving at her parents' house to pick up the kids, her mom was there at the front door glowing at the both of us like the night time moon. I didn't even get the chance to fully get out the car when both her parents came up to me and embraced me in a way I had never felt. "Welcome to the family son", her dad stated. "We decided to keep the kids tonight so you guys can just enjoy this first night as an engaged couple."

I was so happy and thrilled to finally be a part of something but things changed dramatically. All of a sudden, Bailey started seeming to be very unhappy and distant. I have no idea what brought about any of this but I absolutely didn't like it. Suddenly the walls around my heart shot up sky high so that not even God himself could climb them. You know after I put that ring on her finger, it was like her love and affection for me came to a stop. You see I worked at a bar full of drunk women on any given night who surprisingly had no inhibitions at all. I even had someone who worked for me throw herself at me like it was nothing. Every day I went to work the temptations grew stronger and stronger but my love for Bailey also grew and I was able to punch the devil square in the face and tell him this isn't going to work. Don't get me wrong, I was still in the flesh and I would push the buttons by flirting but when it really came down to it I couldn't hurt Bailey at all, I truly did love her. In mid-November despite the issues we were having we got married. Our wedding day was absolutely picture perfect. Granted though it wasn't anything I had ever imaged, I was certainly pleased. You know becoming one with her that day was the happiest day of my life. After we tied the knot, it was all about the new family and God was certainly with us. Blake, her son (and now mine) and I went miniature golfing and to an arcade while Bailey and Brooke took a nap which was a perfect decision. I never thought I'd connect so well with her son as I did that day and I knew that this was Gods working. After our honeymoon night, it was back to reality and back to the deep temptation I called work. This time, however, things were different.

Chapter 10

The temptations were beginning to get so intense over the next two months that I finally broke down and told Bailey about the issues I was having at my job and that I wanted no part of it whatsoever. I got a new job which was actually closer to home with the same pay and significantly less temptations. Regretfully my weakness was still pornography. Since Bailey was going through whatever she was going through mentally, I needed to get it from somewhere and I assumed it would be ok to watch pornography because I thought I really wasn't cheating, or so I thought. My addiction to pornography got so bad that I actually spoke to her mom about it and asked for help. Surprisingly, her mom was very calm and understanding with my faults. After a very deep conversation, she ended up giving me a movie to watch that would help me to understand more the effects pornography had on a relationship. The next few months of our relationship were a blur to me. I woke up and did the same thing over and over not actually growing as a husband or a father until that day in April of 2013. Bailey and I decided we needed to seek a spiritual counselor on our marriage so we went to our church and talked to our pastor about things. There were many issues that were addressed not just from my standpoint but from hers as well. I mentioned this because something happened that day that I will never ever forget. As we left that evening and were standing outside his office, I remember looking at Bailey with my eyes wide and my heart exploding, God had seriously flipped my life and I was ready to fully commit my life and everything associated with it to him. "Bailey I don't know what's going on but I want to give my life to God. I feel him calling me". With a look of absolute surprise and excitement Bailey let out a loud shout "Oh my gosh! Baby, that's amazing. I love you so much I need to call my parents and share this with them". Within seconds, Bailey pulled out her cell phone and dialed her parents. "Mom you'll never guess what just happened? "Bailey calm down. I can't hear you, is everything ok?" "Here I'll let Brian share with you the good news." "Hey mom, how are you?" "I'm ok son what's going on?" "Well Bailey and I just got done at the church and as I was walking out I felt this sensation hit me, mom I'm ready to fully give my life over to the LORD". Man you want to talk about a long silence this was it. All of a sudden her dad gets on the phone and tells me that Annie started crying tears of joy because they had told me that they both had prayed for the last three years for me to finally see Gods love working in me. All the way home that night I was speechless. For the first time since the incident with my childhood pastor, I was back with God and it felt so much better being with him then being against him. Over the next few weeks, both my love for God and Bailey has risen through the roof. All these emotions and feelings were overwhelming but I was able to actually keep them under control. At church in early fall, the senior pastor had mentioned that the church was beginning to form small groups so Bailey and I decided to join one to continue our growth with Christ. That following week after service we went to the meet and greet and joined a group of people similar to our age who ironically were also married with small children. Things were going so well for us. I was no longer at the job where I was tempted, family time was increasing, I woke up nearly every day looking at Bailey and even one day Bailey surprised me a few days after Labor Day after returning from her sisters with something I had asked her for nearly three years, even more reasons to smile.

October 10th, 2013 was the day my name was officially written in the Lambs Book of Christ and I'd have to say with the exception of my wedding day, this was by far one of the proudest moment of my life. In addition to giving my life fully to God, what transpired that day is forever etched in my heart. As I was getting out from being baptized, I was greeted by a good friend who was the first person Id see and she embraced me with a warm hug and whispered in my ear that she loved me and that God loved me too. Now that might sound simple but to me it meant the world especially considering she was just a friend. The most amazing thing that day with the exception of the actual baptism was the reaction I received as I got back to my seat. As I looked at my beautiful wife, mother-in-law and grandmother-in-law all three were tearing up looking at me so proudly. I never, in 30 years of my life, felt so amazing as I did at that moment. I seriously wanted to stop time and live in that moment forever. I kept asking God

"Why did it take so long for you to get me to this moment?" but I couldn't hear a response just yet. The devil was so mad that he no longer had me that he decided to interject in my perfect life. On that following Wednesday, I was laying on the couch just watching some TV when Bailey came home from work on her break. "Brian, do you have something you need to tell me?" As I looked at her lost I answered, "No I don't think so". Then all of a sudden she started to tear up and stated, "So what did you do with my best friend?" All of a sudden my heart dropped into my throat as I remembered what I had swept under a rug and completely forgot about it. I tried to fix this but it was certainly too late. I was so mad at myself but I was even madder that I hurt the woman I loved the most. Throughout the rest of the day, I tried and tried to make things better but one thing about my wife, when she gets her mind on something, there is absolutely no changing it. When she got home that night, she told me she wanted out and that needed to leave. Do you want to talk about going from being on top of a mountain to being six feet under within a day, that's how I felt? Now you see I prayed and I prayed for God to help me but I couldn't hear anything.

Chapter 11

Two weeks after my wife had asked me for a divorce both of our worlds completely crumbled. I was at my brother's house spending some quality time with the kids when I was awoken by an early morning phone call from Bailey crying hysterically. "What's wrong Bailey are you ok?" "Brian she's gone, my mom is gone" A long silence ensued then she told me she had to go and that I needed me to keep the kids all day and I had no objection to that. When I got off the phone with her I got so mad and upset all at the same time at God. I couldn't even begin to fathom why he would take her mother at such a young age. The next few days were a blur to me until the day before the viewing which is the worst day of my life. We were all gathered at her grandmother's house, Bailey, her brother, his girlfriend, her sister Michelle and her husband and his brother, Mr. Township, along with a various number of other friends and family members. Bailey's sister came up to me and asked me if I could watch her son while they all went out for some wine to relax. With everything going on, I was ok with that because I just wanted to be there for them. As I left that day, I approached her sister's husband and Mr. Township and just asked them to make sure Bailey and everyone would be safe and ok despite the conditions. They both looked me straight in the eye and told me they would take care of them so I was ok with that. As I put all three kids down that night a really sick feeling consumed both in my stomach and heart that I couldn't sleep at all. All I could think about was Baileys safety because in the state she was in and the mixture of alcohol, I knew without proper care things could have gotten dangerous and out of control.

      I didn't sleep at all that night and around 6:30, I got the kids up and ready to take back to her house since they had school that morning. You see I knew something was wrong when I got there and the door wasn't locked which when I lived there she had made sure it was locked. Quietly walking into that apartment, my heart was racing but I certainly had no idea why. All of a sudden Bailey came out of the bedroom looking like a complete mess and asked me why I was there so early? "Bailey I told you I'd be here first thing this morning, is everything ok? I couldn't help but get a sudden rush go through my body like a salty knife protruding in my heart. I could remember Bailey standing in the hallway as I walked back going through to our bedroom. To my horror, Mr. Township was lying there half naked on my side of the bed. I remember walking out of that bedroom that morning and immediately out the front door to my car to catch my breathe. Do you know what it feels like to have the devil completely inside you? I sure do because as I sat in my car for that brief moment, the devil was there and enticed me to open my glove compartment, take out my switch blade and proceeded back to the apartment with the full intention of committing first degree murder. As I walked back to the apartment all I could envision was the bloodshed I was about to let loose. When I opened the front door, I felt a huge transformation of the devil leaving and God interjecting. The first person I saw was my step son standing in the living room and he looked at me with fear in his eyes knowing that something bad was about to happen. At that moment, I had suddenly forgotten I had the knife but still proceeded to the bedroom where he was still sleeping. "Wake up, do you know you slept with a married woman and what kind of real man does that while she is grieving over the loss of her mom." By then everyone was awake and instead of scaring the children or committing manslaughter, I left, but Bailey still had the audacity to try and guilt trip me about the kids telling me it was my responsibility to take them to school. I was so angry when I left that morning, I truthfully can't remember what happened for a good portion of that day. That night was super awkward and sad because although things transpired that morning, I still loved her mom and the family. Bailey was introducing me to everyone as her husband and her sister's husband and his brother didn't even show up, so much for support huh? I guess it was ok to have sex with my wife, get what you want but not be there when she would really need you the most? If I didn't have such a love and respect for her mom and dad, I wouldn't have gone. Do you seriously want to talk about a miracle happening even in the midst of tragedy? That same lady who prayed for me feverishly to provide for her daughter and to come to God also changed others as well. The viewing was only supposed to be roughly two hours but when all was said and done it had lasted little over six hours because of the lives she had touched. I have never experienced such an outpouring of love and support than at that viewing. People were coming from all walks of life and even businesses shut down briefly in remembrance of her. I truly believe when she passed away she bypassed everything and instantly earned her wings and became a heavenly angel.

For the next few weeks, I tried my very best to respect Bailey's wishes by leaving her alone but every time I thought I was ok she would contact me asking me if I was going to watch the kids. I still wanted a relationship with them, and her, but I didn't know what to do. Things were actually going ok and even my relationship with the kids was growing but then all of a sudden they were gone. I tried my best to see them or even know how they were doing but I got shunned out of the blue and it hurt me to the core. Again, leaning on God, I just began to pray for her and those kids and just be the best Brian I can be. I began to reminisce about the good times I had with them. What will always stick out to me was when I would come home from work at 3am and wake both of them up to use the bathrooms. I remember this specific instance where I woke Brooke up and she was all sleepy-eyed, wrapped her arms tightly around my neck and nearly fell asleep in my arms. When I tucked her back in she told me, and I keep playing this out in my head, "I love you Step daddy". Man how that girl had my heart and she knew it. As far as Blake was concerned was the last memories I had with him. We would set up campsites and read horror stories and each time, he wouldn't allow me to go back with Bailey and that actually was pretty awesome. If there is one thing I want you to know that I learned through all this is children are the most precious commodity in the world and you need to love them no matter what. You never know when they will be gone! With that being said, the biggest mistake I had made during my marriage and throughout this mess was that I gave every memory I had of those kids back to her because it hurt so much to see that. Ill tell you what though, I had to do it. I refused to be in the middle of her using those kids against me even though they weren't mine. The physical memories are gone but the mental memories are forever etched in my heart. Now afterwards and throughout all this with reasons unbeknownst to me, Bailey's personality flipped. She had become extremely bitter to the point that I was receiving threatening messages about how I was nothing without her and that she was going to take everything I had. Even through this battery of verbal threats, I was still able to shrug it off. On top of all this, my health was also crumbling that it was very noticeable. I went from a healthy 190lbs to a disgusting 140lbs. When I began to realize what was happening, so did the devil. He convinced me and I decided to allow him to begin to fill my head with deceitful things.

Chapter 12

I can remember the day that changed my life forever, Dec 7th, 2013. I was minding my own business then out of the blue Bailey's sister sent me a text telling me Bailey told her that if I didn't switch my cell phone plan that she would have me disconnected. Now you see that situation was so small but because I allowed the last few weeks to build up I thought "It's about time to teach her a lesson." I went to the cell phone store to do what she asked but while I waited, I went on one of the floor phones and sent numerous texts to her claiming I was the guy she had cheated on me when we first started dating. Surprisingly, she believed it because I then texted her from my phone telling her I changed so she had no clue that it was me. She had agreed to allow this guy to come to her apartment for some "fun" knowing he had a girlfriend and she was seeing that other guy. Well I showed up in place of him, and as I did, she was outside waiting in lingerie I had never seen and when she saw me her jaw dropped. She got so mad that when she went back into her apartment, I followed and that's when all hell broke loose. I got so mad at the whole situation but for some reason, I also felt the LORD tug me to do the right thing. In my head I said the heck with you LORD and while she was hitting me to get out, I followed her to the couch and held her arms down but let me make this clear, I did not, nor would I hit her. Well, after a few seconds I snapped out of whatever was going on and left her apartment. Within a few hours, the cops surrounded my house, woke me up from a dead sleep and arrested me for a multitude of charges. I sat in county jail for two days and this was the first time I ever got arrested, wondering where God was at now. Why did he allow things to escalate this much if apparently he loved me so much? Luckily for me, my bond was small and I was grateful that my brother got me out. A week after I got out I couldn't take it anymore and decided it was time to meet God face to face. I devised a plan to take my life. Before I was able to carry out my suicide plan though, my brothers found my stuff and told me I was to admit myself to the hospital or they would. On the way to the hospital that night, I still wanted to die. I was in the backseat with my brother's girlfriend, who ironically was Bailey's cousin. Just as we were flying down the interstate, I was moving towards the door to open it and fall out in the middle of traffic when I felt her hand grab mine and she looked at me and told me "Brian we love you and want you to get better". Those three days I spent in the hospital were a blessing in disguise. While in there, I was served with a restraining order which prevented any and all contact with my wife. At the time I was angry about that, but looking back, I needed it. Next, I was shown a video on suicide and trust me when I say this, suicide is no joke. I didn't know anything about suicide at that moment but then I learned that it affects more than just you, it affects the people who love you even more and I couldn't live with that. After I was released, I truthfully was feeling ok until I drove by her apartment and seen her and this guy on the balcony at 2am knowing the only reason why she's up that late. Now my intentions were to drop the remaining stuff I had of hers in her car but as I did I saw a full set of every spare key she had in her console so maliciously I took them. Over the next few days, I felt an extremely strong conviction to not do anything so I called a mentor of mine and agreed to give him the keys with the intentions he would destroy them but I was wrong. Later that night, I was arrested for violation of the restraining order and sadly this was at 11:50pm Christmas Eve so to add to hurt I was spending the holidays in jail. Again, luckily for me, I was bailed out but the spiritual beating continued. I actually was feeling ok and sorry for everything when I suddenly opened my bank account and it was completely wiped out so my anger rose to a very high level. I went to the bank that day and saw Bailey had withdrawn all my money from my account and later found out she told everyone that it was a bonus check from work so she could take her new fling and friends out to the bars and get drunk on my behalf. You know what though, to some level, I was able to shake it off and finished the year off on a good note.

The beginning of 2014 was ok and I had a lot of faith or so I thought. At the end of February, my court hearing for that horrible night was upon me. On my way to the courthouse that day, I swore I saw the devil and I was scared to death. I remember pulling into the parking lot and for the first time since that night, I seen Bailey getting out of her SUV. When I first looked at her I didn't initially recognize her. Her hair was jet black, skin was pale and had the meanest, nastiest look on her face that I literally was scared to death. I blew off the situation and kept to myself sitting as far away as I could from her in the court room. I have to admit though I kept looking over at her and I realized that this wasn't the person I fell in love with. My lawyer came in and told me that because I told the truth throughout this whole process the D.A. was willing to drop two of the three charges and the only thing that came from it was a fine and two years probation which I accepted. I did what I did and paid for what I did. The next few months of my life were very calm and peaceful that I actually believed the horror movie was over. Boy was I wrong. I received an email from someone very familiar with what's going on but I had never met. Now normally, I don't trust people but this seemed right. She informed me that Bailey was out telling everyone I abused her and the kids and of all things to falsely accuse me of that is the worst. Now for a few days after receiving the message, I needed to confirm that this was the truth. You see unlike most men, I actually pay attention to every detail about someone I love so I knew and remembered all her passwords to everything. This enabled me to hack into her Facebook, email and most importantly her cell phone so everything and more was confirmed. I seen things I couldn't absolutely believe and it not only hurt me but scared me and I didn't know what to do. I can't exactly remember how I got caught but on Apr 26, 2014, I was arrested for probation violation and cyberstalking and had to spend some time in county jail. County jail was absolutely horrible but surprisingly a blessing. While I was in there my mentor and pastor visited me often and kept reminding me that God loves me and that everything will be ok.

During my time, I spent time reading my Bible trying to get right with God and understand what was going on because I certainly didn't know what to do. Through constant prayer and meditation, I was released from jail five weeks later but before I got out my lawyer came to me and told me that Bailey wanted me to sign my car over to her. At first, I didn't want to but after some convincing, I did so. The D.A. could see I was cooperating and was willing to cut me a deal. The conclusion to all this was that

I got hit with two years of probation, my first felony and no contact with her for two years. For the next few days, I was ok but everything I thought was fixed got blew up. I became infatuated with pornography and drinking.

What blew me away though was that nothing had changed with her so all the passwords were still the same. This time, however, what I saw set me over the cliff and I flipped out. First that car I signed over was in turned used to buy her new man a new car which she was even paying his payments. Like I had mentioned before, that's exactly why I knew what each move was going to be because what she did for me she is now doing for him. I remembered back to when for no reason at all my bank account was wiped cleaned so I felt it would be ok to do the same. In one of the texts she sent someone she provided her credit card information with all the security stuff so I used it. I knew that her six month anniversary was coming up with this guy so I sent her flowers and a card from him without thinking about it. The letter I sent had details only mentioned in texts between them, including her "Tango sessions" so I knew that once she found out it that she knew it was me that sent it. She would also know that I knew the truth of what was going on. She made it so easy for me to do this because she did the exactly the same thing to me as she was doing to him with a few minor details so I knew what was going to happen next. This time when I got caught it was what I needed to break me. I was so confused with God and tried to dictate my life by myself and I paid for it. I had called one of my mentors and asked him to pray for God to give me what I deserved and he did.

For the next three months, I battled with the demons in my head, the feelings of anger and betrayal and revenge. I began to start having improper thoughts about her, her sister and someone else that I shouldn't. It was mid-September and my day in court had arrived. I didn't know what I was facing. All I knew was that it wasn't good. The only time I spoke with my lawyer was the day of court and I had no choice but to accept my fate because like day one, I told the truth and was willing to accept my punishment. During my court hearing I listened to what everyone had to say but what stood out was that the D.A. told the judge in front of everyone that I had sent Bailey a letter that said "Your Next" and I didn't do that. They also said that Bailey told them her and new boyfriend were only together for a few weeks when they were together for six months. I was so furious I thought about running out of the courtroom that day and doing something Id regret. As the judge read the verdict, he sentenced me to 15 months in state prison and it was the final blow I needed to finally hear God tell me "Can you hear me now?" The best thing that happened to me that day was I would be sent to a medical prison to seek treatment and hopefully become a different man.

Chapter 13

The journey to State Prison began September 17th, 2014, a journey I was so nervous to embark on. The first day under the direction of the NC DOP was an interesting one. The process was so tedious and nerve racking I felt sick to my stomach the entire day. I arrived at Craven Correctional Institution ready to start this journey. You know my first few days there were hectic and very overwhelming but for the first time since all this had happened, I felt God was with me. Prison wasn't a place for me and especially being a new Christian that it made it more challenging. First off, I had to take medicine for some issues I was having and every single day that I waited in line, inmates would constantly use G.D. or disrespect the staff. Normally I'd shake this off but again I wasn't the same person I use to be so any disrespect of God or humans really made me mad. Day in and day out I had to listen to this and I believe anger was a big flaw of mine that these events were helping me strengthen myself in Christ by not allowing *bitterness, rage, anger, harsh words, and slander as well as any malicious behavior(Ephesians 4:31)* to control me. I promised myself that I was going to keep to myself and not get caught up in "Prison Life" but being confined to a small area, 24-7, you need to adapt to your environment. I still was guided by Christ so I didn't allow myself to get caught up in the illegal activities that were going on so I took my bible, sat in the common room and just read. In doing so, people noticed and a few inmates even joined me. This helped me immensely because throughout this processing in Prison, I was still able to solely focus on the Word. I will tell you though Prison is the devil's playground and I promise you where you are weak Prison will take advantage of it. You see my weaknesses are my anger, irritability, being soft and pornography so trust me I was tested. To start, there are some crooked officers who push and push you because they know they can and that you can't do anything about it. Then you have other inmates who will prowl on you because they you might be weak. A lot of people view me as a nerdy, white boy, and in prison that's a prime target. Everyday for me was a constant battle but I knew I had God on my side and I wasn't at all worried. I was feeling lonely and depressed because I assumed that now I was a convicted felon that no one would love me ever again but boy was I wrong.

I was sitting on my bunk three days into this journey when I received a letter from a lady who I had no clue who she was. As I opened the letter and read its contents I began to see a side of Gods working I'd never seen. This lady was a member of my church whose son was in the same predicament as I was and she was given my information by my mentor to write me. You see this little small gesture started restoring my hope that yes I messed up but it wasn't going to dictate who I was. This letter was so inspiring and uplifting it gave me a spark that I didn't know existed. I prayed and prayed for God to help guide me through this and bring people into my life who would be a positive influence spiritually throughout this journey.

One of the first people I met was a guy we all called "Pops". He was a much older man in for a drug charge but you'd never have guessed it. I slept on the top bunk while he was on the bottom so we had the opportunity to speak often. This guy was like a father figure to me. You see I didn't have money on my inmate account and in prison you must fend for yourself for food and supplies. Grant it they do feed you three meals a day but they aren't filling and at times absolutely disgusting. Pops would buy me little things to survive on and in addition what he wouldn't eat he would share with me. A few days into it while minding my own business a guy we call "Plug" approached me to talk to me about scripture and his problems. I mention him because when I first saw him I felt like punching him in the face because he looked identical to the guy my wife had an obsession with. After speaking to him we actually had a lot in common and he was a good person for me to interact with and talk to about God with. Now you see prison wasn't just about the good people, there were people in there who would try to exploit you using everything they could. I can remember this guy who was from where I lived and he started sharing the word with me and even gave me a better Bible. Later that night he tried to guilt trip me into buying him things because he talked to me about God. While reading the Bible and working on my writing another guy asked me to borrow a stamp and that he'd replace it in the morning. You see in prison stamps are very valuable and used for any type of dealing. Getting that stamp back was key not because I wanted to deal but because I loved writing people and they were very hard to come by. I waited and waited for him to replace the stamp but one day he told me he wasn't paying me back so I got mad. In prison this is called "getting debowed". I promised myself that under no circumstance I would never be a victim again. I decided to "swoll up" to him and he backed down but I certainly left the impression that this wasn't going to happen again because it didn't. Now people have this impression as though prison is a dangerous place and grant it some places are but where I was during processing was ok. I did however experience a gang war in the yard which was overwhelming. One of the biggest issues in prison is gangs and on this day the Bloods and Cripts joined together and jumped an Arian Brother but surprisingly the Arian Brother held his own and got the best of them.

Unfortunately because of this altercation and for the safety of others, the camp was put on lockdown for three days. My life became difficult because at this point I had shaved my head and was automatically labeled an Arian Brother so every time I saw a gang member I was confronted and had to prove myself. One of the many blessings God had proved for me was my old roommate from county jail was also transferred to this facility. JT as we call him was very much into the Word and every day in county we talked about God. In addition he taught me a lot about the bible which I was so grateful for. He was like my big brother and I believe he was brought into my life to teach me not only about God but not to judge others, especially in prison. One thing I wasn't use to having to be on was a schedule. Everything in prison was on a schedule and there was no compromising to it. For example, inmate count occurred at 530am, 2pm, 5pm and lastly at 10pm all of which no matter what you were doing you had to stop and either stand by your bed or stay exactly were you are at. You meals were at the exact same time even if you weren't hungry which can be difficult at times. The menu was the same seven things every single day of the year just in different rotations. Since I was in processing I had to endure a plethora of tests to assess my mental, physical and psychological capabilities. To my surprise, the doctors throughout this process were able to assess a few things that doctors on the outside weren't able to.

First off, they found my heart to be beating irregular and after some other work was done they would inform me if I had a heart murmur. I then was given a bunch of tests to measure my intellectual capabilities and the results were just as I had already known. I tested high on English but wasn't very strong in math but that's nothing new to me. Lastly, were the psychological tests I went through. Of course they concluded that I had high levels of anxiety and depression but something I wasn't aware of is that I struggled with controlling my anger. You see, I'm not a violent person and wouldn't hurt a fly but I tend to get angry quickly. I was afraid that if I bottle it up too long that I will explode which I hope to never get there. I have learned how to control myself and how to channel things through God who sees me through everything. Everyday that past something was always testing me. In prison you tend to be able to focus on things that in the real world you wouldn't normally think about. For example, my dreams were absolutely crazy that they either would make 50 Shades of Grey blush or make someone cry water works.

No matter what had transpired, my heart was still with my wife and those kids. You see I struggled letting go which was partially the reason why I ended up here so I promised myself to just let go. Every time I thought I had let go Id have some type of dream resparking any bottled up feelings I had. It especially hurt me when I had dreams about the kids. One night before I fell asleep I asked God to let me know how they were and that night I had that dream. I dreamt that they were ok but before I woke up they both gave me a hug and I remember it like it was yesterday they said "Step daddy, we will always love you". Those kids may not be mine and I may never see them again but in my heart they are and always will be room for them. As far as Bailey is concerned the dreams were mixed. During the days I was angry I had hurtful dreams reliving that fateful night. On the days when I was relaxed the dreams I had were priceless. I don't know nor do I care but the dreams were never of sexual intentions and I believe that's because I finally got to a certain level of love for her that hadnt yet been discovered. I had so much free time on my hands going through processing that I began to realize a lot of things that I was doing wrong in life and sadly the people I had hurt. It was certainly a gut check I wasn't ready for but was glad it was happening. I spent an awful lot of time thinking and for me was dangerous but at this point in my life I was able to take my thoughts captive by the renewing of my mind(see Romans 12:2). As much as I hated being in there I felt safer in there then out in the real world. There were two memorable things to happen to me in processing that I believe was God talking to me. The first event was the guy I told you about earlier they called "Plug". He came up to me out of the blue and wanted to talk. He kept talking how his faith was fading because of the issues in his life and how he didn't believe God really loved him. I looked him straight in the eye and told him to quit talking like that and that God does love him and that he is a child of Christ. Now I wasn't as confident in my walk as I am now but I had extra material from my pastor that I had shared with him and his reaction on his face was priceless. I did notice a tear formulate in his eyes but he hid it well because crying isn't something to do prison no matter what you're feeling. The weird thing about that was that same night he got shipped out and I haven't seen or heard from him since. The next issue, and probably most powerful I had experienced was a guy they called "Josh". He also pulled me aside and told me that he and his mom were able to lead someone back to Christ just by them living their life according to faith. Now you see that might not seem major but if you knew Josh's background and the background of this girl you would see that as always God used bad to deliver good and to me this gave me so much hope. People have a serious misconception of those who are in prison. Just in processing I learned a lot about a lot of people and yes maybe some got over on me but that's no different then how people do things outside in the real world. You see because of the lessons I learned with my marriage and growing up I am more easily able to differentiate between real and fake. You see every day that I spoke with God I asked him to deliver away bad company and surround me with Godly influences even in prison.

The journey through processing took roughly two weeks and then I was finally transferred to my permanent place for the next year at Hoke Correctional Facility. Before going to Hoke we stopped at what is called the "Bullpen" which was a central meeting place for inmate transfers to their assigned locations. The bullpen was packed I mean wall to wall people in such a little space. Being there, we were given a bagged lunch which was totally disgusting. Once I got on the bus, I headed to my next location and said goodbye to the old Brian. To try and mess with me the devil allowed the trip to drive by the scene of my crime not once but twice and to know what I knew that was going on there made me sick to my stomach. You want to talk about something scary though. As we pulled up to this facility and no lie it seriously looked like an abandoned mental hospital that you see in horror movies I was starting to worry. I mean even going through the required pat down I thought this was it. I don't know if it was just me but I seriously felt death all around me and this wasn't something I was comfortable with. I was placed in the South Housing unit which I later learned was prison's equivalent to "the hood". I was given a flat mattress that was like sleeping on a sheet of paper and I had to share one bathroom with nine guys and two showers with nearly 100 others. Over the next few weeks my adjustment to prison was difficult.

Chapter 14

So is it a safe bet to assume that as you're reading this, you believe what you have seen on those prison TV shows about prison life? Prison, unless you're in medium or closed custody, is absolutely nothing like that. You see though prison is what you make of it. For me, I was blessed to be in minimum security as well as a medical camp which lessened the violence than other places. Most of the people who were at this facility had petty crimes and the ones who were there with murders and such have been down so long that they kept to themselves. The first room I was designated too was like living in government housing. The facilities were beat up; there were ten people per room with only two showers for the whole block and the heating system was broken. You see when you needed "things", the hood was where you'd find it. I had seen countless deals happen daily which also lead to multiple confrontations like the kind you see when things go sour. I'm not going to lie, I was a very quiet until I came in there. I quickly learned how to adapt but certainly was not comfortable with it. The tv situation in this room was truthfully the biggest issue. Each individual had different interests of what they wanted to see but there were two guys who basically controlled things whether you liked it or not. One thing I learned though is that there are battles just not worth fighting and what's on tv is one of them. I learned to adapt to not having tv by burying myself in more constructive things such as reading the bible, writing and working out. I was blessed to have a guy in the bunk next to me who was in the same mindset I was so we both looked out for each other. Now you see there were two guys who were in there that singled me out and thought they would "get over" on me. I can remember them trying to tell me what I was going to watch on tv so this made me very mad and I was still in my revenge mentality so I fought back the only way I knew how, by deception. You see everyone slept throughout the day and I was up bright and early so I stole the remote, programmed what I wanted then hid the remote so they couldn't do anything and were stuck. You should have seen how humorous it was to watch grown men freak out over a remote, I admittingly took pleasure in it. It didn't bother me one bit because I worked, wrote and read all while they freaked out. Looking back it was wrong of me to do this and I do feel bad but at that stage in my life I didn't care. I was in the mindset where no one tells me what to do. I let this go for about a week and then I hid the remote somewhere where I knew they'd find it but know I didn't do it. I was blessed to only have to put up with that room for a short period of time because since I had a job in the kitchen.

Chapter 15

First and foremost I needed to find a job which I was able to do in the kitchen. You see I wasn't blessed with money on my inmate account every week or phones calls or even visits so I had to do things to survive. I started off in the kitchen making $.40 a day, seven days a week, around six hours a day. A prison kitchen isn't like anything you'd ever see in the outside world. The kitchen had certain rules to follow and if we as inmates were to disobey we would get fired and lose what is called "gain time". Gain time is time you work to get your maximum sentence down to your minimum. In my case the judge gave me a 15-27 month sentence which in reality is actually 15-18 with 9 months post release (a.k.a parole). In order for me to work down my sentence I had to keep this job and work for 6 months because in the kitchen you get one month off your sentence for every two months you work. My first job was as a janitor and that in other words was the utility person.

Luckily for me, I served desserts which were the most sought after position in the kitchen. I learned it was also the biggest headache and would certainly test my anger and patience. You see the rules simply state that you're only allowed a single portion but with dessert, people were trying to hustle or intimidate me into giving them more than their fair share. I wasn't having it so I swolled up and told them "NO," and you know I couldn't tell you how many people threatened me but nothing happened EVER. I was pushed around all my life in the real world and now I was in prison it was time to push back. You see this might not have been the smartest thing but I figured if I can "toughen up" in prison, reality would be so much easier. I prayed to God to open a door for me before I say or do something I'd regret and within two months he delivered me to a new position, away from the headaches and where I can just keep to myself and that was lead dish man. Here I earned a dollar and really only had to work at serving time which I was completely fine with. You think the headaches stopped? They actually only got more intense. See in prison, inmates are very manipulative and will lie, cheat and steal as much as they can. The kitchen supervisors knew I was an honest person so they warned me about how items from the kitchen would be slipped out the dish room window and if something was then I'd be accountable for it which again how fair was that? For the first month I was back there, I was tested. I was not in there to be anyone's friend or homeboy but everyone thought they were because I was a godly man. Anytime someone tried to sneak something I put a halt on it and it caused a lot of people to get mad but nothing happened because of it. Grant it, if I was in medium or closed custody, I would have lost my life but I didn't feel fear whatsoever and I needed to not show weakness and it worked. Grant it every so often Id be tried but nothing that I was worried about it. You see my relationship with God was strengthening so I knew he was there to protect me. These events didn't make me a popular man but I was ok with that. I was in prison to get better not increase my popularity. People began also seeing that God was the center of my life and because of this it lead me to people with similar interests which helped pass the time.

I am the type of person who utilizes every resource that is available and in the kitchen I had additional resources to help me grow. Working out and writing were two of my favorite hobbies. Here is an example of the poetry I had wrote during my tenure. Keep in mind I was angry and confused and although they aren't perfect poems, the four line verses was from the heart.

Dear My Lord and Savior Jesus
Please rid me from this pain
I want to be a child of God
And not go insane

As I struggle with these demons
Both internal and external in my life
I ask that you please
Watch over and protect my wife

Do you know someone who stole your breathe
And wouldn't give it back
I would give anything for that someone
And that's a well-known fact

Why do people make me angry
And think it's funny when I'm in pain
God I try to do what's right
What do they have to gain

I use to think my marriage was a waste
However I learned a many of things
Never give up on love
And the way the heart will sing

Every day I struggle

Is it really worth the fight

I believe it is

Because one day I'll see the light

Woman always judge me

Because I'm quiet and shy

Little do they know

I'm a really nice guy

Walking in the house that day

And seeing you in bed with another man

Really hurt my heart

But now I realize it's all a part of Gods plan

As the days grew older

And your heart even colder

Just know I'll keep my promise

That you can always cry on my shoulder

I'm not afraid of anything or anyone

If it means protecting the ones I love

Because I got someone stronger on my side

And that's the man above

I have been to jail
And even through divorce
It's given me the strength
To take the world by force

When I was stuck in PA
During the late of winter
I never could image
Behind that smile was a heart so bitter

Before I fell in love with you
I had no soul
My life was in control
From the man below

I know I made you promises
I'll do my best to keep my word
I can't do this without you
Please please please help me Lord

Step Daddy we love you
Is the sweetest kind of chatter
But unfortunately you were taken away from me
Which caused my heart to shatter

The devil use to be my friend
And gave me everything I wanted
Until one day I realized
I was the one being hunted

You can push me away
And tell me it's not worth the fight
But I'm following my heart
Its telling me to do what's right

Alcohol was my candy
And sex was like my drugs
But the only thing I really needed
Was a simple bear hug

You know what's really sexy
When you wake up looking like death
To me you're so desirable
Ill kiss you even with morning breathe

Want to hear something funny
I miss your pretty toes
Will you and I ever be
Only God is the only one who knows

No matter how much I lift weights
You is who makes me strong
Being with you my love
Makes me feel like I belong

You fixed me when I was broken
And took care of me when I didn't feel well
But through the faults of both of us
We stumbled and we fell

I hate seeing you hurt like this
And not wanting to fix the past
All this will catch up with you
Causing the pain to forever last

There will be many times
When we fight and disagree
Just know that I love you
You mean the absolute world to me

I picked up and dusted off
But you continued to still be broken
Baby please wake up
Here comes the locomotion

Beyond a reasonable doubt
Life will eventually catch up to you
So really think about fixing your past
That's the best thing you can do

How can I forget
You know I'll always remember
That day we became one
That cool day in November

Here is my heart
I've enclosed it in a locket
Keep it around your neck
And not in your pocket

Your body is like a drug
I've become an addict
But you becoming my wife
Has got me really frantic

People are jealous of me
Because wife is hotter
She's so smoking sexy
I've got to drench her with water

In my heart
There's an open place
For you to occupy
So come take up that space

As I take you home tonight
And gave you a good night kiss
I then looked to the sky
And thank God for all this bliss

Come into my arms
I want you very near
You're the one I want to be with
I can't be any clearer

I can try to put how I feel into words
And they'd create a beautiful love song
There is no one I'd rather be with
You're the one for whom I long

My sadness has been mounting
Because of what I did with Melanie
Now because of my actions
My record has a felony

Addy is my little baby
She will always be my honey
Thinking about her
Makes my life a little runny

Ill always be there for you
You possess my heart
Nothing is going to stop me
All we need is a proper restart

Someone asked me tonight
What's the secret to life
I said it's knowing God
And a very beautiful life

Every time I close my eyes
All I picture is your face
I'll respect your wishes
And give you your space

With the time passing slowly
I try so hard to live
Let's just let go of the past
And learn to forgive

Everything will be alright
I'm going to make this right
I'll never give up this fight
One day ill kiss you goodnight

I hate playing this game
Things will never be the same
My heart begins to shatter
Every time I hear your name

If dreams depict your feelings
Then mine say I'm sorry
To hide from all this pain
I started a personal diary

Some people will say
It's all about the base
Guess what I fell in love with
Your pretty gorgeous face

My idol and inspiration
Has taught me to seize the moment
To pursue my dreams
And become an award winning poet

I use to think
Our lives were a fairytale story
Until that day in October
When you acted super horey

As the holidays pass
Id have to let our a big sigh
Guess its time
To say goodbye

My life was a crumbled mess
I could never do what was right
Until God took my hand
And said son Ill protect you in this fight

Waking up this morning
I feel a whole lot lighter
God helped me conquer this pain
And turned me into one his prized fighter

2014 was absolutely terrible
But when I realize about my story
All I can do is look to the man above
And give him all the praise and glory

The days were looking bleek
But looking to God I got back my smile
He never gave up on me
So I just chalked this up under "Gods miracle file"

Our souls were one if you must know
And never shall they part
With splendid dawn, your face aglow
I reached for you and found my heart

Through all this pain
And constant struggle
Please come here baby
All I want to do is cuddle

Dear LORD and Savior Jesus
Thank you for dying on the cross
Releasing us from our sins
And showing Satan whose boss

You know I did all I could
But its hard for me to let go
You know Ill always love you
Why…because I said so

Ill never leave you nor forsake you
Or give up in this race
Your heart is what I covet
Its the prize for first place

Ive asked the LORD above
What in the world do I say
To help you back to Christ
And all he said was to pray

Thinking about a family
All I can do is spectate
Id give anything
To be an active participant

Laying here in bed
Thinking a lot about you and the kids tonight
Hoping and praying
That everything will be alright

My tears fall like rain
Id give anything to hear your name
Thinking of my life without you
Brings me an immense amount of pain

Sitting here Im missing my family
My dog, father and brothers
But no one more
Than my mother

Im tired of living a life
Tired of being someone Im not
But what tires me most
Is the people I never loved a lot

Never take for granted
What God gives to you
Denying his love
Will make you a fool

I miss my little girl
She was the apple of my eye
I promise to never give up
Im going to see her before I die

Then there was my buddy
Everyone calls him TC
I might have been the step daddy
But I considered him my son, you see

Being with the one you love

Makes you feel alive

But without you

I don't think I can survive

My Life has caused me pain

You can even bein to see what Ive been through

Because throughout our relationship

Its been all about you

To CAT:

Why did God take our backbone

When he took your mother

RIP CAT

You weren't like all the others

You accepted me for who I was

And helped me beat my flaws

But not having your guidance

I have broken many laws

The last words you spoke to me

Were to love and protect your daughter and kids

Don't you ever worry mom

That's all I ever did

We might have lost an angel

Its hard not to cry

I love you CAT

For this isn't goodbye

To "Bailey":

You can't hide from the past
It will catch up to you fast
Without facing it all
You certainly will never last

No more hurt
No more pain
For you there's so much
More to gain

I did all I can
To be the perfect man
But all you did
Was picked up and ran

One thing I know for a fact
I won't let you crack
Till death do us part
I'll always have your back

To "Blake":

To my little buddy
Step daddy favorite little man
I'll always love you buddy
And be your biggest fan

I'm so proud of you
You're such a tough little guy
I'll never turn my back on you
Or even say goodbye

Don't ever give up
Always put up a fight
God will take care of you
Just keep doing what's right

Mommy and Brooke
Need your protection when I'm not around
Don't ever be sad though
Cause ill easily be found

To Mr. Township:

My mother in law

Well she was a hugger

Keep trying to screw with my family

And you'll feel the wrath of a Louisville Slugger

I'll turn my back

And spare your life

All you got to do

Is stop f**** my wife

If you chose not to listen

Ill have to throw down this rod

And give you over

To my almighty God

You claim to be a marine

And live by Sempre Fri

So you better love her and those kids

And never ever make them cry

To Mr. Township:

Bailey you have no idea
How much I think you're pretty
All I know is he is a joke
I'm the capital and he's a small city

What in the world is this
I can't believe what I'm seeing
A man sleeping with a married woman
All while she's grieving

You claim to be a man
But all that I can see
Is a helpless little baby
Who's trying to be all he can be

God will take care of you
For that I know for sure
I'm going to stay on the straight and narrow
So my life stays pure

<u>TO NOEL:</u>

You sell cars for a living
And try to make a hustle
You tried to get my wife drunk
Now I'll show you my muscle

I'm glad I wasn't around
But I read every word
For your sake
Get on your knees and pray to the LORD

You call yourself a friend
But all you are is an abuser
Telling my wife to leave the kids to get drunk
You piece of crap loser

I'm in prison for a year
Because of the mistakes I made
Come around my wife and family
And I'll cut you with a blade

To Mr. P:

I had a lot of respect for you
Until you got into my business
This conversation isn't over
Because I'm going to finish this

I understand you're a friend of the family
And always had their backs
But before you open your mouth
Make sure you know all the facts

Did you really think it was your place
To keep track of where I'd be
Well I was getting right with God
For that you didn't see

I'm going to let this slide
Trust me I'll do my best
But next time mind your own business
And let this all come to rest

To "Bailey":

Explaining the hurt that you delivered
Telling people I beat you and those kids
God will take care of all this
You and all your fibs

The little ones might not be mine
But I'll love them until I die
I'm going to do all I can
So they don't need to cry

Saturday morning cartoons were the highlight of the day
Watching them sleep was the best at night
No matter what happens to me
I wont give up this fight

Earthquakes rattle the world
And fires will burn
But my love for those kids
Will last as long as the world turns

<u>To Kio:</u>

We have been friends for many many years
And I can truthfully say you never brought me tears
I'm sorry I haven't always been around
But open your heart that's where I can be found

You were so young when we met
But all my promises for I have kept
Ill always be there for you until the day I die
You can surely count on it for I do not lie

I admire how much you always did your best
Through all of life's problems you have passed the test
Addy and Greyson are your precious little bugs
Maybe one day we can all have a group hug

I'll finish off by saying good luck with Brett
I'm pretty sure he loves you for that's a fact
But in case I'm wrong don't settle for less
I'll always love you and be here to clean up any mess

TO THE EXTENDED FAMILY:

Most people call you paw paw
But Ill call you dad
Please forgive me for what I did
You know Im not that bad

Dear "Michelle" there is so much I can say
I hope you can forgive me Ill begin to count the day
My words came from anger that's certainly not a fib
I felt that you intentionally hurt me but what was is that I
did

"Cal" you little guy I wish I wasn't so shy
We could've been bros but someone stepped on my toes
Please take care of her now you maybe be the only one who
hears my heart sing
Good luck with the lady she's an awesome catch I bet we
all know she's the best vet

To everyone else I can't explain how I feel
I can't believe it got to this it's all so surreal
One thing I can promise is that my love will forever last
I've forgotten the hurt and turned my back to the past.

So back to prison life in the kitchen. While I was working and if I wasn't writing poetry, I would complete my necessary tasks and then use buckets filled with water and ice to work out with. In prison, you need to make do and be creative with what you have so I did. The great thing was that you weren't really allowed to but I was able to earn the respect of the kitchen supervisors so they would "turn their heads" if they saw me do it unlike the trouble makers where they would keep them busy. One of the best things to working in the kitchen was having first dibs on the food and anything left over. The bad thing was that you saw how the stuff was prepared and regretfully it was absolutely disgusting. I was in that kitchen for nearly six months and the menu never changed just the days changed. You want to talk about having gratitude for food, try living on prison food for a year and your eyes will be opened I promise. You see even though prison food was disgusting it was also healthy for you. I went into prison weighing a staggering 140lbs but upon my release I was up to a healthy 170lbs. At one point I got obsessed with wanting to get huge I nearly topped out at 200lb but saw what it was making me look like and I didn't like it.

Chapter 16

The best thing about this location was my new living quarters in the central dormitory. The central dorms were like the Hamptons of that facility. You see each block had forty people but it was two to a room and four showers per block. There were also two TV's, one designated for movies and the other for sports/news. Most people in these blocks had medical conditions, worked in the kitchen or were just simply quiet. My first cellmate was a challenge because he didn't like white people and only had one leg so he felt like the world owed him something. Again at this point, I was already in prison for four months and had adapted my own routine so he didn't bother me whatsoever. There were a few days where he challenged me but I believe this was part of God's plan for me to help grow me as a Christian and love everyone as God would love them. I prayed and prayed that God would lead me through this roommate situation and he answered my prayers. About a month after becoming roommates with him, he ended up transferring to a new facility and that same day, I got a new roommate. This roommate was a great choice and again God delivered which I am grateful for. He worked first shift in the kitchen (I worked second) and by the time I got back he was already asleep. When we did cross paths, we actually had really good conversations about God and he even felt comfortable with me to confide in my with some of his personal issues that he was dealing with. I tried to get him to be more open and not stay so hidden in the room where it would drive you crazy if you let it and you know he eventually did. I felt so good about this because in my prayers I ask God to put me in places where I can help others and this was my first chance. You would be surprised how just saying hi to someone can really open their eyes and heart. The next five months went by fairly fast with him as a cellmate but his time was over before mine and he got released. I was grateful for the time spent with him. He not only opened my eyes to some things I never knew or understood he was also an ear for me when I was having a bad day. That same day he was released, I got a new and final cellmate, who was very odd but quiet and kept to himself. He also worked first shift in the kitchen so we hardly saw each other as well but when we did we were cordial. This guy had a lot of pent up anger and had no one on the outside to communicate with.

Most of his time he spent angry or sleeping but yet again I believed God put him there for a reason. You know I wasn't blessed with much while I was in there but with what I had I really tried to help others. I can remember one instance I made some wraps and I offered him some and something about that gesture really opened his eyes. He ended up breaking his silence and from that moment on didn't shut up. He might have had a lot of things going on in his head but the look in his eyes at the gratitude he gave me for just being nice really showed me how far being nice can actually go. Prison had a lot and I meant a lot of angry, hateful people within those walls and it's really sad to see that most people avoid these people when in actuality we should embrace them. Now you see in prison that's an awfully difficult thing to do but who cares, what's the worst thing that can happen? In the time I was there I did experience a lot of amazing fellowshipping just because some people just weren't scared. Being scared isn't something that comes from God. It says in 1 Timothy 1:7 *"God has not given us the spirit of fear but of power and of love and of sound mind"* and personally if it's not from God I don't want it. One of the good things of being in this section of the prison where most kitchen workers were, I was able to interact with a few of them. The guy I mostly interacted with was Bobby. Bobby was a genuinely nice guy but unfortunately he just made a stupid decision like I did and was also a first timer.

Now in prison you need to be very careful listening to what people's crimes are because a lot tend to try to act all tough when really they are. Bobby was in there for something really dumb (like me) but if you initially saw his charge you would think he was a heinous person. It was weird, I felt comfortable talking to him and every day we would hold each other accountable for the LORD. We would ask each other questions and call each other out if we weren't living according to the Bible. You see with Bobby though, the one thing that ate me up inside was how incredibly spoiled he was. Every week he would have $40.00 on his account for canteen, phone calls to family, letters and visits once a week. I never held this against him but it hurt. You see in the 15 months I was away I got three visits and had to beg for everything else. What was the most amazing thing though was the letters I received. When I went away, I prayed for God to take away all the people in my life who would be a deterrent to my spiritual walk and replace them with God-Fearing ones. Do you think he delivered? Of course he did. While away, I had only received letters from my dad, a few from my brothers but the majority came from my church and from most people who didn't even know me. I don't know what happened but it hurt me a lot to not receive any letters from any other family members whatsoever but when they needed me I was always there. The letters I received were so absolutely heart-wrenching. I received a letter from these two ladies who I didn't know at all and they told me how they are praying for me but what really hit the heart was that after I had responded they both wrote me back telling me how my letter inspired them. There was no way in hell I was about to let prison or my past tell me what my future was going to be. You would be surprised at how a letter can really impact someone's life. You see though I didn't receive a lot while I was in there, when I did, I was extremely grateful. In addition to working, there was only one other thing I did in there that was pleasurable and that was working out. I became so obsessed with it that when I wasn't reading the bible or family books, I was working out some type of way. I thought to myself that I seen all these stories of how people went to prison and came out all huge so I wanted that.

Prison was surely filled with meat heads so I was bound to learn something that I could apply to working out and boy was I right. I met up with this guy who was down for eight years and he was absolutely huge I mean double my size and all muscles. Take a wild guess how I ended up learning from him? I simply saw him sitting by himself and looking really depressed so I introduced myself to him and a very brief conversation ensued and it was history. He was down in the dumps about his family and how he missed out on his children growing up, lost his wife and lost his mother to cancer just a few months prior. He was in there for assaulting someone with intentions to inflict serious injury and ended up paralyzing this guy all because he caught his wife having an affair on him. You are probably thinking "Wow" but I was blessed because God brought this guy in my life to help me too since we had something in common. His was more violent than me but if I would have initially acted I could be where he was. I will never understand why God allows people to come in your life but I learned not to second guess him. We talked for about a week about God, the bible and he vented to me about a lot of personal issues he was dealing with. Talking to him really instilled an appreciation for God's grace and mercy, for my family and for life. Tomorrow is never guaranteed so make sure your tank is empty at the end of the day. You wouldn't want to go to heaven on a full tank now would you? So after a few weeks, I took the next step and we got on the subject of working out and his face lit up like a child's on Christmas. You can see that working out was something that was very pleasurable to him and to be able to now have someone to share that with showed it really met a lot to him. I can remember going out to that weight pile that cold morning and seeing that this venture was going to be one heck of a ride. We worked out together for almost five months and in that time, and in the time I spent myself, my bench went up 75lbs and I gained nearly 40lbs. You see before I came to prison, I was really depressed but was still working out and in the matter from the night my wife did what she did to my first day of prison I lost 60lbs and looked disgusting. I made a promise to myself to get back to the healthy me so in addition to continuing to work out I ate everything I could. At my peak I gained back those 60lbs and almost hit 200lbs until I realized it was fat and really not muscle. After I met this guy, I was able to trim up and ultimately get down to a solid 160lbs with complete satisfaction with my accomplishments.

Chapter 17

Every day was a personal battle for me. For one, I had trouble forgetting about my wife and the kids. The biggest difficulty wasn't the fact of what happened, it was what I was feeling was going to happen. No one realizes what I saw and read that caused me to lose it. I just knew in my heart something was wrong. I was slowly coming to an acceptance that she and the kids were gone but what I couldn't grasp was the fact it seemed that everything that happened was all on me. I lay in my bed nearly every night wondering where things went wrong and all the what ifs that a relationship can have. I had taken classes to become a better husband and father, I turned my head when she cheated on me the first time and I even let go when she told me it was over. Again, it still wasn't ever good enough. I was so angry at her and then it lead to me succumbing to my addictions. You see the first six months that I was away; I couldn't care less about things but then things started to surface. I fell deeper into depression so I did the only thing I knew that would make me happy. The dreams I had in prison were crazy. I can't explain why but unlike out in reality, I could remember them in very vivid detail after I woke up. Most of my dreams were good and pure but I'll tell you what, when they were dirty they were filthy. Now you would think that this would be a problem, I took it as a blessing. Since I was more aware of what was going on in my life and the works God was doing, it wasn't so difficult for me to throw out those impure thoughts. I do have to admit there were moments when I didn't know how to throw the bad thoughts out but I was blessed with an amazing pastor and mentor at my church who helped me through that. I don't know how to explain the occurrences but many times as I would be struggling with things, Id receive a letter from him or from someone at the church confirming I was loved. Just the thought of that let me know that things would be ok. I learned to develop an extreme disliking for television so as I mentioned before, I'd journal or write whatever is going on in my life at that moment. I wrote countless amounts of poetry, religious material, as well as the book your reading right now. You see I began to realize that the devil really doesn't mess with people he already has and just that simple fact that I was being spiritually beaten everyday lets me know I was getting closer to God. One of my many weaknesses in life is that I'm very quick to anger but when I get angry I bottle it up. Every single day that I was incarcerated, I was tested. I fit the typical stereotype of the dorky white boy in prison. People thought I was in there for Tax Fraud or something and you see I was in there for a computer crime which I guess fit me into that stereotype. At the time of incarceration, I was also very soft spoken and kept to myself, again solidifying the stereotype. There came a point, about four months into my 15month sentence, I just threw up my hand and said to myself that if I was going to toughen up, this was where I am going to do it. I didn't care if I was going to have to take a beating or increase my time. I vowed not to be bullied anymore. For 15months I stood my ground and gained a lot of respect from people who otherwise wouldn't have any for me; I even got the respect of the Correctional Officers. What's funny is I couldn't have done this if God wasn't in me. My growth spiritually helped me to grow as a man and I'm forever grateful for that. The bible does say in Psalms 23:4 that *AS I WALK THROUGH THE VALLEY OF THE SHADOW OF DEATH I FEAR NO EVIL*". Yes there were times I was nervous when I confronted or was confronted by inmates. I also knew God was with me that whatever would happen would happen.

For the longest time, I couldn't realize where all this newfound strength was coming from but then I realize where it did. I was corresponding with my pastor and he sent me something about forgiveness and for some reason it really hit me. For the life of me though, I couldn't understand what it meant. That night while saying prayers, I asked God to please explain to me what this meant because I thought all I needed was to say "I forgive" and that I wouldn't have to think or worry about specific situations anymore. After about three days of constant prayer and meditation, God finally spoke to me. In the library I found a great book on Forgiveness and divulged in it. In addition to the book, I had come across a scripture in *Matthew 6:14.* In there it stated that *"For if you forgive others their trespasses, your heavenly father will also forgive you (ESV)".* I started applying these lessons that I was learning and it was like opening a door to a house during a fire; that was how powerful the blow was to me. I couldn't even begin to fathom the hurt and pain that I had bottled up for thirty years and I began to genuinely weep (and in prison you need to hide that). Do you want to talk about the flood gates opening up, that's exactly what was going on in my life at that moment. I seriously started to remember everything from all the way back when I was six years old until the present moment. Anger had a strong hold over me that I never knew existed and it destroyed me life. Day in and day out, I prayed for God to reveal to me who I needed to forgive. I sat up for the longest time and made a list and when I tell you this, the list was long and detailed, no joke. I couldn't even begin to image when all was said and done the amount of people who hurt me and I hurt from something so small to things that in some cases were beyond being normally forgiven. It took honestly the length of my sentence and constant prayer to finally release a lot of that hurt I had felt throughout my life. Forgiveness is very key to getting rid of that excess baggage in your life. True forgiveness is to believe in someone more than they believe in themselves...to have faith in them even when they have lost faith in themselves.

In addition, to forgive is to let go of your ego, to forgive is not to accept someone's actions, but to accept them as humans. True forgiveness is empathy, a way to peace and harmony at it's an action of highest compassion. True forgiveness is an acceptance, of our own self, for what is it that can be reflected in others that can't be found in us? True forgiveness begins with forgiving oneself first. If you ask God to forgive your sins, that's very good, yet only one part of the equations. When you truly, and finally forgive yourself first, then forgiving others kind of falls into place. What I mean by forgiving yourself, is to relieve yourself of any negative thoughts or emotions about you. Maybe just forgive yourself of guilt for having these negative emotions. Or, maybe forgive yourself, in the sense that you don't want to have any connections whatsoever, of who wronged you. You need to be free and clear in your mind and spirit of whatever it is that is bothering you. To free yourself is to forgive you and all others involved. True forgiveness could harbor no resentment for wrong doing, an acceptance of the other person just as she or he is, in this moment, you've let go of yesterday, and you are as one with the other and can only experience compassion and love. Forgiveness is the acknowledgement of the element of God in every person and offering honor to that. And lastly, forgiveness is to cease feeling resentment against another who has wronged you or someone else. To no longer feel negative emotions about a person who has wronged you or someone else for whom you care. To put the wrong behind and in the past, and to move on with your life is my definition of forgiveness.

Chapter 18

There are things that I encountered that are absolutely hard to just forgive but that's when it's the best time. You may always hurt because of what someone else did and that's completely understandable. When you are able to forgive you release both parties from that and God takes it from there. Its not our job to judge one another. Its says in *ECC 3:17 that "in due season God will judge everyone, both good and bad, for all their deeds".* No one ever listened to me but I listened and paid attention to everything people I cared about the most would tell me. Looking back on my life, the people who hurt me the most are the people I loved the most. While away I realized never to turn my back on anyone because if they will stab you, let them muster the courage to do it in your heart, not your back. Never in my life would I ever had thought I'd explode like I did but once again when I seen what I seen, all those years had just let loose. My suggestion to anyone who is reading this, DO NOT BOTTLE THINGS UP, you will thank me later. The weirdest thing happened to me though during all this. God was at work in my heart and although I was a new Christian, the devil still slightly had a grip on me and I didn't realize it. I knew God was working but I assumed Satan wasn't around, big mistake. You see as it's summed up in *Romans 7:14-25*, I was trying so hard to do right by God when I should have been trusting him. God loves me so much especially at this moment that he allowed certain events to transpire and truthfully I was mad at him for it. I gave my life to him and this is how he repays me but then to see the love my dad and church still showed me continued to provide me the hope I was looking for. I was struggling but once I got to prison and I quote a very great inspiration to me Mr. Ray Lewis of the Baltimore Ravens. He said, and I realize I got the same message, that I was sitting in prison and I finally heard God say "Do you hear me now" and I dropped to my knees. Do you want to talk about a conviction; this was certainly one heck of one.

For the duration of my sentence and continuing today as I write this, God is my number one priority not my option. I understand why things happened as they did and I am absolutely grateful for this. As I corresponded with my pastor and a family member of mine I kept asking them "why did God wait all this while to get me to this stage of my life". Do you know what they both said (and yes they both answered exactly the same). They told me "You weren't ready" and I believe it. It would be scary if nothing wrong was happening and Im blessed it does. Every so often in prison, I was getting upset because I was missing my church family and being involved but guess what, God delivered again. You see prisoners think their lives are over or not worth living but we are actually loved like everyone else. In the little over a year that I was behind bars, I had met some of the most amazing people involved in the religious community that even when I doubted life they somehow were there to pick me up. God was using them to keep reminding me that I was loved and he will never leave me nor forsake me no matter what the circumstances. I can usually spot a fake and grant it there were many, in my eyes, but also learned that its not about the messenger, its about the message. As much as I was into the bible, these individuals assisted me in learning more and understand God on a whole deeper level than I had ever expected.

As I mentioned before, I did keep to myself but keeping in the word, God had delivered to me a group of genuine "God-Fearing men" who I was able to relate to. Trust me when I say this. When you give your life to God and ask him to take away things that might hinder your growth he will listen. Now understand this might involve family or people who have been around forever but in the long run as long as you keep your eyes on him he will replace them. If you're lucky, he might even bring them back better than they use to be. I suggest that if you want something like that pray for them and worst case scenario you may never see them but your prayers will help them help someone you know? You remember when I had mentioned earlier in this book about my addiction to pornography? While in prison, I thought the chains of that bondage were broken but in reality they were just loosened but I was still locked down.

Chapter 19

The moment I got out, Sept 14th, I felt so freed that I will admit I did venture to my old ways but God wasn't having it. First off, I logged onto social media and contacted a few individuals and go off where we left off before I ventured away. As hard as I wanted to fight it, God again wasn't going to allow me to be defeated. With one certain individual she basically threw herself to me and the old Brian would have acted without a doubt but something inside me wasn't having it. This girl was so persistent until it came to the point where I was willing to lose a friend than put myself in a tempting situation. For about a week, the devil kept enticing me but every time he did, God had my back and I'm so grateful. Another mistake I did and even to the day I am so sorry for was that I told someone near and dear to me the dreams I had while I was away about her and I was very descriptive about it. Now luckily for me, God helped me work through that situation and restore any damage that might have been done because of my actions. Do you know when the devil can't get to you in the flesh, he will use other outlets to defeat you? For me that was the internet. For about the first two months, the internet was so easily available and he kept feeding me telling me how what I was doing wasn't a sin because I wasn't participating in premarital sex or hurting anyone and I believed him. Again God interjected and made me feel absolutely horrible afterwards where it got to the point where I was so disgusted with myself. It also came to the point where I couldn't look at a woman without feeling horrible about it. My sex drive became destroyed that for a while I couldn't even force a dirty thought whatsoever. Truthfully though, I was so proud that things were progressing but as always the devil wasn't having it and I suddenly got lazy in my walk with Christ. He brought an old fling into my life and regretfully I lost all control of myself and took what was given just because I thought since it had been over three years that something bad was going to happen to my "equipment" if I didn't. When I left that night, I looked up to God and felt so horrible that I ruined all his work over the last three years. You know what was even more horrible about that was the fact that the devil used my past to anger me so I wasn't thinking straight at all and I knew it. He kept feeding me with thoughts of that horrible morning seeing what I had saw and thoughts of every girl I had ever hurt or who have hurt me with the subject of sex. Do you know that it is actually physically possible to hate something so bad that it scares you and that's how I felt about sex? After I was given that conviction, I began to abstain from anything that would even trigger a slight feeling. I stopped watching TV, only used my phone for calls and texts and consumed my thoughts by God. I prayed every day for continued strength and as always the devil wouldn't let up just this time I was equipped to fight back. I can't even begin to express to you how much of a relief it is to not have to battle with sexual temptation anymore. I use to live and die by it for nearly 20 years and now I frankly don't care about it. I am able to look at woman with more respect that wondering how she would perform you know. Now don't get me wrong, I know and understand the temptations are always going to be there but I am now more aware of them. I take myself out of any situations that might pose even a slightest problem and run to the truth. You'd be surprised how much a little change can make a huge difference.

I was so happy to no longer be under the control of the NC Dept. of Corrections but was horrified for the unknown. Here I was fresh out of prison and nothing to protect me but I did have the faith that my God was not going to leave me nor forsake me. First I was blessed that my youngest brother and his girlfriend came to pick me up but as always the devil seized the moment. You see my brothers' girlfriend is also the cousin to Bailey so even though it wasn't intentional just the sight of her resparked some of the fears and anxieties I had. It wasn't a good idea seeing as though I was so fresh and raw out of prison that I couldn't even have a second to adjust before the devil was ready to pounce. When I arrived back at his house, one of the greatest things in the entire world had happen. As soon as I opened that door my dog Rocky started loving on me like I've never been loved before. Do you seriously want to talk about a great feeling that certainly came pretty close to being the greatest feeling ever? I didn't care what was going on at that moment; I was going to love on him and try to make up for the time I had lost while I was away. The first few days after my release were fairly busy but God certainly provided me with an ample amount of blessings. Being a convicted felon I thought it was going to take me a long time to find a job but I was able to land a decent job at a local sub shop only three days after I was released. In addition to that, my brothers allowed me to use their vehicles to do what I needed to do. When that wasn't an option, I took an hour bike ride to work for the extra cardio work I missed during the day. You see Im very much into fitness so driving that five mile one way didn't make much difference to me either way.

When I wasn't working or at the gym, I enjoyed spending all my free time at the church just helping out. Being there I felt safe and for the first time since I moved to NC, I felt like I belonged somewhere. My mentor took me under his wing and did everything he could to teach me about God and help me to understand that, in his words, "I am Gods child and that he really does love me". In addition to teaching me things, he also brought new "friends" into my life to help me even more on how to become the man I needed to be. There were multiple occasions where he would call me just to check on me and times he would ask me to lunch just to spend time with me. Im not sure as you are reading this you understand the magnitude of those simple actions but to me they were a HUGE! What really touched my heart the most was that he was there anytime I needed him and he has been since the day I left his office with my then wife? When I went to court multiple times, he was there. When I was sitting in county jail, he visited me at least once a week. When I was in state prison he wrote me every other week and also provided me information to other members of the church who wrote me as well. I truly believe that the amount of love that showered me during my most difficult times was exactly what was needed to weaken the chains that were holding me from a life of happiness. You see even when I was released I was still welcomed at the church and not judged because I was a convicted felon. I battled constantly with the perception that I was going to be shunned away and have no where to go but I was truly wrong. My relationship with the church is so amazing I cant even put into words. I have no doubt that my life is far from where it use to be and even now when I struggle it doesn't hurt so much. Since my release I have become more actively involved in the church and the relationships formed in the few months since my release are more valuable to me than most if not all the relationships I ever had. Something worth noting and can only be a working from God. I was sitting in church one Wednesday night in the same spot I sit in every week. For nearly two months no one acknowledged me but on this one particular day, Angela and Josh, one of the two couples sitting near me, decide to introduce themselves to me which broke down any walls that were built up around my heart. You see every week the same people sit in the same spot so you tend to form relationships, not me though. I have a very high level of anxiety in meeting new people, especially people who I feel are better than me in any aspect of human life. The people who sat around me I learned were two couples, Mitch, a police officer (ironic seeing as Im a felon?) and his firefighter wife Jennifer in addition to Josh and Angela who for some reason I felt so gravitated too but also very intimidated by. I was completely blown away that this lady would even consider talking to me not to mention introducing me to her group of friends. One thing I had forgot to mention was that for the last three months I kept asking my mentor who these people where because I really wanted to be friends with them but certainly felt absolutely inadequate about it. When this lady broke that chain, I almost teared up it meant that much to me. To be able to finally start getting over the fear of talking to people who I felt inferior to was can only be God helping me through this. Even as I am writing you this, the relationship I have with the two guys is better than most relationships I ever had. The devil doesn't like that because every day he tries to get into my head trying to convince me that I'm still not good enough and that how can a convicted felon be friends with a State Police officer? Of course I still am of the flesh but it's not that tight of a stronghold any more like it used to be. As a matter of fact, I will be going to lunch with the officer today and maybe through the strength of God be able to form an even tighter bond. You see since the bond was broken by the simple actions of this one lady, I was able to open up even more in the church and join a group of people in my age range. These people share a lot of the same interests as I do and in the short time I've been involved a few have even motivated/inspired me. It worth mentioning that again the devil tried to steal my joy but through prayer everything worked out. Its so weird because these events and Sunday school with this people are very overwhelming because of my anxiety but like the bible says in Deut 31:6, *God will never leave me nor forsake me* and he's kept his word. I am able to break out of that comfort zone and introduce myself to others but I still struggle immensely with approaching woman. I have all my life to break that fear and in time that chain will be broken.

Chapter 20

Throughout this experience, I began to see the true importance of the family dynamic but none more so that within my family. As you have read previous, I had a working relationship with my parents but there really wasn't that strong foundation of love. My experiences in prison and the excessive amount of time I had to think and pray truly took off those blinders that were stopping me from moving on. First and foremost was my relationship with my father. While I was away, I prayed and prayed for God to see me through this and of course he did. I mustered up the courage to write my father a very extensive, in-depth letter expressing to him my thoughts, feelings and emotions that had festered up over the years. Do you want to talk about feeling so much lighter emotionally, I sure did after sending the letter. I'm not quite sure what exactly happen, but after I had sent that letter the relationship with my father has strengthen and to this date it's the best it's ever been. While incarcerated, I receive a letter from him at least once a month and he helped me out on multiple occasions with both financial and miscellaneous information such as addresses and documents. Just that little stuff he did over the short time I was away helped prepare me greatly for a smoother transition back into society. The greatest thing he does now is he actually calls me at least once a week to check in and tell me he loves me which he NEVER did until all this happened. I know its hard for him to do this but its way better late than never. Now you see on the other hand my relationship with my mom disappeared. I was away for nearly two years and in that time I never received a letter and grant it for Christmas she sent a card and put money on my account which I was grateful for but it was like her and my dad switched rolls. Image sitting in you prison cell hearing about how everyone is receiving letters from their moms and not receiving one of your own; that kind of hurt. In the last three years, I might have heard from my mom three times if that and in reality that's just not supposed to happen. It hurts me an awful lot to know and feel that my mom might not love me anymore and I hear her say it but I've also learned words mean nothing if there is no actions behind them. I do understand, and I'm not making excuses, that we are not her biological children but she still is my mom no matter how much I mess up. It's like I was a good kid all these years and she was readily available but I mess up and I'm now the ugly step child. It messes with my head and makes me think the only way I can be loved by anyone is that I have to be perfect.

In addition to my parents, I was blessed to have some great, but pain in butt brothers who I love a lot. My middle brother James is just a year younger than me. My relationship with him is unique in a way. Each time I was arrested, he was there to post my bail and believed in me not to mess up again. When I was incarcerated he actually came to visit me as well as when I needed money he placed money on my account which I was very grateful for. Now what really touched my heart was that he stayed in North Carolina and took care of my baby boy Rocky. Rocky is my rock and if anything was to have happened to him I would have never been able to forgive myself so him looking after Rocky I was truly blessed and grateful for. My other Clyde was the youngest and the brother we both lived with. My relationship with him was very unusual however. You see I am very much into my relationship with God but he is the complete opposite and at times we clashed majorly. Clyde was a very unpredictable individual and I never really knew what to expect on a daily basis. I know he has a great heart but it's so hard that I just wasn't sure how to handle each outburst. On top of it all, his girlfriend is related to my wife and I just felt so uncomfortable around her. You see when I was released I truly did my best to not think about my wife whatsoever but every so often her name or a memory or something would come up to cause me to reminisce and I hated it. Every day that passed and my relationship with God increased the devil was getting madder and using them to hold me back from excelling. Day in and day out I had to battle them someway because they thought since I lived there that they could control me which wasn't going to happen whatsoever. After living there for nearly three months, it got to the point that if I didn't leave or something was going to happen that I would regret. Throughout this whole process, both of them knew that I was on parole and any little mistake I made I could go back to prison. For reasons I will never understand they pushed every button. After I had left though, I was able to get my own car, save money, focus more on my three huge goals but most importantly become closer with God. Don't get me wrong, I am grateful and always will be for what they both did but sometimes if you want to grow, you need a healthier environment and being there just wasn't in my plan. On top of wanting to grow I needed to separate myself from his girlfriend because I needed to just let go of my wife and let her be. I needed to strengthen my focus on God (and my church), fitness and accomplishing my dreams and goals. I dearly love and miss my brothers but I've done all I could and hope my new relationship with Christ shows to them and they see that a life with God is the only life to live.

So your probably wondering what happened to my marriage since that horrible night aren't you. Every day as I sat in county jail as well as state prison, I thought and wondered how she was doing. I could have filed for divorce for only $1.00 or so I was told but my heart wasn't telling me to do so. My feelings were so strong that I had to journal them or I would have exploded. The horrible thing the devil tried to key on was everything I read and seen prior to getting arrested and trying to convince me it was all my fault. In reality, I do accept half the responsibility but I certainly don't accept it all. There were people I knew that actually kept me updated on how she was doing but once I got to state prison I stopped all that because I had come to the conclusion I just had to surrender her to God and let him do what he needed to do. The craziest thing was that I had this dream in Jan 2015 about her which when I woke I was sweating and in absolute tears. In the dream she was laying in our bed convulsing like she was possessed and I was calm, took her hand and placed it her heart and simply stated "I love you" and "I rebuke you Satan in the name of the LORD Jesus" and he left her body and became the woman I had fallen in love with three years early. When I was released, I did slip briefly and looked at her email because the passwords were STILL THE SAME but boy did I feel a conviction from the Holy Spirit. After seeing what I saw, I knew she was beyond humanly help and did nothing with what I seen and simply in my heart said see you later. I came to the realization that I had really needed to just let go, never stop loving, but just simply let go. She is an absolutely amazing, beautiful, sweet woman but she's not the woman I fell in love with. She's a true fighter but until she loves herself, I mean truly love herself, she won't be able to give anyone the love they needed, including her kids. I've never met someone who was so beautiful both on the outside as well as the inside but because of past hurts that inner beauty is tarnished and needs some polishing.

As I come to the conclusion of this book, I really have some sort of a different perspective on life. First, I was able to make peace with a lot of my past personal hurts weather I hurt or was hurted. I no longer possess anger or revenge and really it makes a world of a difference. My urges to partake in watching pornography or even having random hook-up are really strong but I have been blessed with the spirit so I am able to fight off those urges. It's so amazing because I asked God to help me appreciate woman more and he delivered. I don't view them as objects or means of my "tension release" but more like human beings who need to just be loved and appreciated without any ulterior motives. I also look back at all the triumphs and tragedies I had endured and have come to the realization that this all a part of Gods grandest plans for me. I was so mad for the longest time wondering why the heck it took God so long for my life to evolve into what it is today and in simple words, PATIENCE. I understand and accept that life will never be easy but to have God with me that's all I will ever need. My perspective on life is much broader and more appreciative than it's ever been. I was taught by my mentor and my senior pastor to ask God to open your eyes to see things the way he does and oh boy does he if you ask. I see things in people that most people take for granted. I see things in my surroundings that most people overlook or if they see it they truly don't grasp the magnitude and significance of the specific thing. If you receive anything from this book I want you know that I truly love and care for each and every one of you. In my opinion the three keys to a successful life are faith, forgiveness and failure. If you have the faith that God is the almighty creator and that he is always with you know that fear will never destroy you. Forgiveness is not just to the people who hurt you but also forgiving yourself is a very key component to both your spiritual and physical well-being. I tell you from personal experience, when you come to the point of forgiveness, the weight off your shoulders makes you feel so much lighter (ha to those of you self-conscious forgive others and yourself and see how "lighter" you become). Lastly you need failure as well. I have got a master's degree in failure but it lead me to get my PhD in success. Something did happen to me that Im glad happen and Ill end on this. At a service after I got out, my pastor asked the question, "If your partner was to be in an accident and you would have to take care of them for the rest of your lives and never be intimate again, can you still love that person and be with them forever? That really had me

thinking and well I realized a lot, kind of scared me. So in

conclusion, love is just not a word, its an action! Think

about it. God bless and love you all!